DOUGLAS DC 10

P.R.SMITH

Copyright © Paul R. Smith 1990

First published 1990 by Airlife Publishing Ltd.

British Library Cataloguing in Publication Data
Smith, P. R. (Paul Raymond), 1966–
    The DC-10.
    1. McDonnell Douglas DC-10 aeroplanes, history
    I. Title   II. Series
    629.133349

    ISBN 1 85310 086 2

Printed in Singapore by the Kyodo Printing Company (Singapore) Pte Ltd.

Airlife Publishing Ltd.

101 Longden Road, Shrewsbury, SY3 9EB, England

Introduction

It hardly seems possible that it is more than twenty years since the Douglas DC-10 was in its planning stages, and the sales team were trying to generate sufficient interest to guarantee the aircraft's launch. That this was accomplished was an achievement in itself, but to beat the rival design, the Lockheed L-1011 Tristar, into the air, was indeed a remarkable feat. Sadly, it was the events that followed that tended to obscure this success, which was replaced instead by a reputation for being somewhat accident prone. The media lost no opportunity to record every incident, no matter how small, involving the DC-10. It should be noted that in the majority of cases the aircraft was not to blame, but some other factor, such as pilot error or weather conditions. In saying this, however, there was cause for considerable alarm in the case of the faulty cargo door and the resultant THY disaster in France. It is obvious that this accident should never have happened and it was another two years before a solution was implemented.

Ironically, it was another Douglas product that also suffered its fair share of accidents in the early post-war years. It seemed that every transport which either crashed or was damaged was a Douglas DC-3 Dakota. This fact was quickly pointed out by the media, even in those relatively early days of aviation. What was not noted was the fact that there were many of these aircraft built, and a large number of them were flying safely throughout the world. Even today, some forty years on, quite a considerable number of DC-3s are still flying.

With the introduction of the wide-bodied airliner, cheap air travel became possible for an increasing number of people. There is, of course, no doubt that the DC-10 was responsible for playing a major role in this revolution. A staunch advocate of this type was Sir Freddie Laker, whose Skytrain project and its accompanying publicity brought the aircraft firmly into the limelight. As soon as the long battles were over, the trijet's success on transatlantic crossings forced other airlines to lower their fares to compete, and in some cases, change aircraft type. As you read this book, many millions of passengers have been flown, in complete safety, on DC-10s around the world, on millions of flights. Many of these travellers never actually get to see their aircraft due to the modern airbridge systems in operation worldwide. In any case, once inside, one wide-bodied aircraft looks much like another to the untrained eye. Thus, such is the acceptance of modern air transport.

When the final Douglas DC-10 was rolled off the Long Beach production line in March 1988, destined for Nigeria Airways, it was the 385th civilian example of the aircraft. Indeed, it is remarkable that production was continued for so long. This was due to the USAF generating the work for an order for sixty KC-10A Extenders, the last of which was completed at the end of 1987. As the production line was cleared, the way was paved for its larger sister, the MD11, and the first of this type was rolled out in the last quarter of 1989, an inaugural flight taking place in the early weeks of 1990. It is hoped that this aircraft type will achieve even greater success than its predecessor, with hopefully none of the bad publicity which dogged the DC-10.

TABLE OF COMPARISONS		
	DC-10-10	DC-10-15
First flight date:	August 29 1970	January 8 1981
Max. accommodation:	380	380
Wing span:	47.42 m (155 ft 3 in)	47.42 m (155 ft 3 in)
Length:	55.66 m (182 ft 3 in)	55.66 m (182 ft 3 in)
Height:	17.74 m (58 ft 1 in)	17.58 m (57 ft 6 in)
Max. t/o weight:	199,545 kg (440,000 lb)	206,387 kg (455,000 lb)
Max. cruis. speed:	925 km/h (501 mph)	925 km/h (501 mph)
Maximum range:	7,894 km (4,260 miles)	10,317 km (5,571 miles)
Service ceiling:	12,800 km (42,000 ft)	12,800 km (42,000 ft)
	DC-10-30	DC-10-40
First flight date:	June 21 1972	July 25 1975
Max. accommodation:	380	380
Wing span:	50.57 m (165 ft 3 in)	50.57 m (165 ft 3 in)
Length:	55.45 m (181 ft 6 in)	55.66 m (182 ft 3 n)
Height:	17.74 m (58 ft 1 in)	17.74 m (58 ft 1 in)
Max. t/o weight:	259,457 kg (572,000 lb)	259,457 kg (572,000 lb)
Max. cruis. speed:	908 km/h (490 mph)	922 km/h (498 mph)
Maximum range:	10,140 km (5,475 miles)	11,112 km (6,000 miles)
Service ceiling:	12,800 km (42,000 ft)	12,800 km (42,000 ft)
	KC-10A Extender	
First flight date:	July 12 1980	
Max. accommodation:	80	
Wing span:	50.40 m (165 ft 4 in)	
Length:	55.45 m (181 ft 6 in)	
Height:	17.74 m (58 ft 1 in)	
Max. t/o weight:	267,619 kg (590,000 lb)	
Max. cruis. speed:	922km/h (498 mph)	
Maximum range:	7,038 km (4,373 miles)	
Service ceiling:	12,800 km (42,000 ft)	

AEROMEXICO (AM/AMX)   Mexico

The airline, known until February 1972 as Aeronaves de Mexico, was established in 1934 and began operations between Mexico City and Acapulco in September of that year. Since 1952 several smaller Mexican airlines have been taken over, including Lamsa, Aerovias Reforma, Aerolineas Mexicanas, and Guest Aerovias. In 1959 Aeronaves was nationalized and the Pan American holding passed to the Mexican Government. In 1970, under a Government plan, Mexican domestic airlines were rationalized into an integrated air transport system under the control of Aeronaves de Mexico, and organized into eight smaller carrires. Aeromexico, one of the country's two national airlines, and now renamed Aerovias de Mexico, but still marketed under its former name, was declared bankrupt in April 1988 by its owners, the Mexican Government. The carrier has been considerably over-staffed for some years, and an attempt the same year to reduce costs provoked a major strike which grounded the company. A state-owned company was appointed liquidator and took control of the airline's operations, drawing up a six-month recovery plan in preparation for privatization. By the end of this period services had been restarted to thirty domestic destinations and five US cities, but overall a slimming down has occurred. A sixty-five per cent controlling stake in the airline was acquired in November by Gruppo Dictum, a consortium of Mexican business interests. The Mexican pilots' union, ASPA, has purchased the remaining shares. With Mexicana, Aeromexico has the distinction of being the other operator of the DC-10-15, the variant that was designed for operations in hot climates and high altitudes. Three Series 30s are also employed, and are maintained on the routes to New York (JFK) and Miami. Prior to the bankruptcy, they were also operated on the Madrid and Paris (ORY) sectors. A fleet of DC-10, DC-9 and McDonnell Douglas MD82 aircraft is maintained, along with several examples of the DC-8-51, although all of this type has been withdrawn from service. The latest Aeromexico livery, which was introduced in the early eighties, is simple yet attractive. A highly-polished natural metal fuselage-finish not only forms the perfect backdrop for the broad bright orange cheatlines, but also pays dividends by saving a considerable amount of weight, and subsequently, fuel. White 'Aeromexico' titling in lower case lettering, complete with an accent over the 'e' of Mexico, appears near the forward passenger door and on the third engine of the DC-10s, below the famous Mexican birdman motif. All fleet members wear a similar livery apart from DC-10-30 N3878P, which is unique in having a white fuselage base colour, with the rest of the design unchanged. The carrier's ICAO call sign is 'AEROMEXICO'. *(Aviation Photo News)*

AIR AFRIQUE (RK/RGA)

Ivory Coast

Air Afrique was officially constituted in March 1961 by an agreement between eleven independent states, which were formerly French colonies, and the Société pour le Développement du Transport Aérien en Afrique (Sodetraf). Operations began in August of that year. Air Afrique's first Douglas DC-10-30, TU-TAL, was delivered in February 1973. It entered service to take over such routes as the Dakar-Marseilles-Paris (CDG) and Abidjan-Nice-Paris (CDG). Two more of the type were delivered between 1975 and 1979, allowing some of the busier African sectors to be covered by the larger capacity aircraft. Subsequently, with the arrival of Airbus A300s, there was a degree of over-capacity in the fleet. Leases were negotiated with various airlines, and the aircraft have seen many liveries. In October 1980, Air Afrique purchased a Boeing 747-2S4F SCD, for use on its pure freight services. Gainful employment was found until March 1984, when a series of leases saw the end of its service with the African carrier. The aircraft is, at the moment, in service with Korean Air, as HL7474. Each of the participating states contribute 7.2 per cent of the capital, while the remainder (currently 28 per cent) is held by Sodetraf. Distribution of the initial share-holding changed with the withdrawal of Cameroon (in 1971) and Gabon (in 1976). Today the company operates an extensive network of regional services within Africa, and serves a number of destinations in Europe. New York (JFK) and Jeddah are also included in the carrier's international network. At present the airline is 72 per cent owned by the following states: Benin, Burkina Faso, Central African Republic, Chad, Congo, Ivory Coast, Mauritania, Niger, Senegal and Togo. A fleet of Douglas DC-10, DC-8 and Airbus A300 are currently operated by the airline, as well as, at the time of writing, a Lockheed L-1011 Tristar Series 1 on loan from American Transair. With the large number of nationalities involved with the carrier, it was a logical step that the livery of Air Afrique should make use of natural colours. Thus, bright shades of lime and emerald green were chosen to colour the board cheatlines. Simple 'Air Afrique' titles are displayed on the white roof in black upper case lettering. However, the livery's *pièce de résistance* is its ethnic tail logo, which symbolizes the far-reaching services by using a gazelle's head. This spans a stylized globe, in a matching shade of emerald green. The carrier's ICAO call sign is 'AIRAFRIC'. *(K. G. Wright)*

AIR FLORIDA (QH)   United States of America

Air Florida was founded in November 1971, and with a base at Miami Airport, Florida, began passenger services within the state on September 29, 1972. It was deregulation that was responsible for Air Florida's growth rate in 1979, its route network expanding almost daily. Likewise, its fleet of aircraft was unable to cope with the linkage of numerous airports down the eastern seaboard of America. At the time when National Airlines was subject to a takeover, Air Florida was one of the interested parties. The main purpose of its interest was to try and prevent a merger with Eastern, its rival on so many routes. In any event, it was Pan Am that won, but since both parties already had licences to operate over the lucrative Miami-London sector, the FAA decreed that another carrier would be nominated in addition to Pan Am. A total of ten airlines applied, nine of which were, to say the least, amazed to find that Air Florida was a serious contender. However, most observers thought that this time the airline had over-reached itself. To enable the Floridian carrier to gain experience of the DC-10, the carrier leased N1035F, a Series 30, from Seaboard World, delivery taking place on March 13, 1980. Two weeks later, the aircraft commenced work on a charter programme. This was based upon a total of 134 round trips to Europe, of which fifty per cent were centred on the UK and the Netherlands. The single DC-10's utilization increased when permission was granted to fly scheduled services to Amsterdam and Brussels in May and June respectively. The airline then campaigned vigorously for the London licence, until it eventually emerged the victor. The sole DC-10 was no longer capable of undergoing such a heavy workload, so a further three examples were leased from Transamerica,

deliveries of the first pair being in time for the launch of the Miami-London (LGW) service on April 3, 1981. It proved to be an immediate success, but by the year's end the situation did not look so good on the domestic scene. With excess capacity, higher fuel bills and lower fares, these factors became part of a steady reduction in Air Florida's seemingly non-stop expansion during 1982. Transamerica took back its DC-10s, upon payment of a penalty fee, but since the London route was one of those that was actually making a profit, alternative equipment was sought. Following an interim period whereby a selection of Boeing 707s were used, a pair of World Airways DC-10s were leased in the spring of 1983. These aircraft came on far more favourable terms than before. Unfortunately, their assistance was inadequate to restore the earlier successes of the carrier, which in July 1984 was obliged to file for bankruptcy. Prior to this, Air Florida operated scheduled services to fourteen cities in Florida, to Toledo, Ohio; New York (LGA); Boston, Massachusetts; Burlington, Providence, as well as to Georgetown, Rocksound, North Eluthera, Treasure Cay, Marsh Harbour and Freeport (Bahamas), Santo Domingo and Puerto Plata (Dominican Republic), Belize City, Tegucigalpa and San Pedro Sula (Honduras). In addition, services were operated to Brussels, Amsterdam, London (LGW) and Shannon. A fleet of DC-10-30, Boeing 727-200, 737-100 and -200, and DC-9-15 types were operated. An order was outstanding for three Boeing 757-2T4s, although due to the aforementioned reasons, these were never delivered. The carrier's ICAO call sign was 'PALM'. *(K. G. Wright)*

AIR NEW ZEALAND (NZ & TE/ANZ) New Zealand

The national carrier of New Zealand was founded as Tasman Empire Airways, a joint British-Australian-New Zealand company (owned 20:30:50), formed to operate services linking New Zealand and Australia. In 1954 Britain withdrew, and in 1961 the New Zealand Government assumed full ownership of the airline which, on April 1, 1965 adopted the present title. McDonnell Douglas delivered Air New Zealand's first DC-10-30 in early 1973, an event marked by the adoption of a new company livery. As more of the type were brought into service, the aircraft took over the international routes to such points as Singapore, Tokyo, Vancouver and Los Angeles. An agreement with British Airways extended the latter service through to London (LHR) from 1975. It was this development that justified an order for a further three aircraft. Eventually, Air New Zealand maintained a fleet of eight DC-10s. In 1977 the Government decided to merge the two state-owned domestic and international airlines. From April 1, 1978 New Zealand National Airways and Air New Zealand were amalgamated under the latter name. NZNAC was formed in 1945, beginning operations two years later. Associated companies of Air New Zealand include Safe Air (100 per cent holding) and Instant Freeline Reservations. The airline also has a 77 per cent stake in the Mount Cook Group, as well as a 50 per cent

holding in Jetset Tours. In the early 1980s, following a rationalization programme, Air New Zealand's entire DC-10 fleet was sold. Today, the company operates an extensive network of scheduled passenger and cargo services to twenty-four main domestic points, while international routes link Auckland, Christchurch and Wellington with points in Australia, the Far East, USA, Canada and Europe. A fleet of Boeing 737, 747, 767 and Fokker F-27 types is maintained. It was decided that the old Air New Zealand livery, introduced over five years prior to the merger, would be retained in preference to the somewhat overpowering orange and red of NZNAC. It is this scheme that appears on all aircraft fleetwide. Twin 'straight through' cheatlines in deep blue and turquoise underline blue 'Air New Zealand' roof titling, which appear in a bold typeface alongside the national flag. This refined colour combination, evoking images of the Pacific, is repeated on the fin to form the backdrop for a traditional Maori symbol, known as a 'Koru'. Seen here is DC-10-30, ZK-NZN, whilst on its final approach to London Heathrow's Runway 28R, on June 1, 1975. It should be noted that it was to this airport that Air New Zealand operated before being forced to move to Gatwick Airport. The carrier ICAO call sign is 'NEW ZEALAND'. *(B. J. Eagles)*

AIR ZAIRE (QC/AZR)   Zaire

The Government-owned national airline of the huge African state of Zaire was formed in June 1961 as Air Congo, and adopted the present title some ten years later to coincide with the country's independence from Belgium. Air Zaire was, surprisingly, an early customer for the DC-10. The first (9Q-CLI) was delivered in June 1973, having been part of a cancelled order from the German company Atlantis. It was joined, a year later, by a second. The pair then operating the carrier's long haul schedules between Kinshasa and Paris (ORY), Brussels, Rome, Geneva and Zurich configured with 252 seats. An extensive network of passenger and cargo services to over twenty domestic points from Kinshasa and Lubumbashi, together with international services to Abidjan, Libreville, Lomé, Dakar, Conakry, Luanda, Brussels, Paris (ORY), and Rome. Major shareholders are the State (80 per cent), Institut National de Securité Social (eight per cent) and the Caisse d'Epargne du Zaire (eight per cent). A fleet of Douglas DC-10-30, Douglas DC-8-63 and Boeing 737-200C aircraft is operated. On order for delivery during the 'nineties are three McDonnell Douglas MD82s, and two McDonnell Douglas MD11s. The company's livery consists of a straightforward red windowline, which is trimmed either side by yellow and green pinstripes, all colours appearing on the national flag. Black 'Air Zaire' upper case titling dominates the cabin roof, complete with umlaut over the letter 'i' of 'Zaire'. When Fokker F-27 Friendships were utilized, these wore titles on the lower fuselage, for greater visibility. The tail fin sports a stylized 'winged-leopard' motif in gold within a red circle, and the whole of the rudder is painted bright green with a small red band near the top, trimmed in yellow. The leopard is the traditional symbol of Zaire (animal to 'honour'). The livery was designed within the airline, and is based upon the colours of the national flag; this — consisting of a field of green with a yellow disc in which appears a black arm carrying a red torch — appears on the forward fuselage. The current livery was introduced in October 1971. Prior to this date the aircraft opreated as Air Congo using a similar livery but with the aircraft's rudder in blue, not green. Seen here at Paris Le Bourget Airport, in June 1973, is 9Q-CLI, the carrier's sole DC-10-30. 'Mont Ngaliema' was originally with UTA, as F-OCQC. The carrier's ICAO call sign is 'AIR ZAIRE'. *(Aviation Photo News)*

ALITALIA (AZ/AZA)

Italy

Alitalia, the Italian national flag carrier, was formed in September 1948 under the name Aerolinea Italiana Internazionale (Alitalia), in associated with British European Airways. Its aim was to operate converted war-surplus bombers over a domestic passenger network, which began the following May. In 1948, the first international flights, to the Argentinian capital Buenos Aires, took place. The present title was adopted in October 1957 when, with the backing of IRI (the present major stockholder in Alitalia), the company was merged with Linea Aerea Italiana; which was then Alitalia's main competitor. The Italian airline's subsidiaries include the domestic carrier ATI, and SIGMA. In November 1985 Alitalia sold thirty per cent of its 780 million preferred shares, and floated nineteen per cent of its common shares. This reduced the Italian Government's ownership from ninety-nine per cent to around seventy per cent. The airline operates a worldwide network of scheduled passenger and cargo services from Italy to points in Europe, Africa, North and South America, the Middle and Far East, and Australia. In October 1986, Lima (Peru) was added to the network. In July 1986, Alitalia and CAAC launched a joint Beijing-Rome (via Sharjah) service, initially using the latter company's Boeing 747 aircraft; although this has subsequently changed. A fleet of Boeing 747, Airbus Industrie A300, Douglas DC-9, McDonnell Douglas MD82, Piaggio P166-DL3, and SIAI Marchetti SF-260 aircraft is maintained. At least six McDonnell Douglas MD11 Combi types are on order for delivery in the early 1990s, as well as a number of Airbus A321s. Seen here at McDonnell Douglas's pre-delivery area at the beginning of 1973 is I-DYNA. The aircraft, a Series 30, was delivered to Alitalia on February 6 of that year. 'Galileo Galilei' served the airline well, until December 1982 when it was sold to the Boeing Commercial Airplane Company in exchange for Boeing 747 equipment. It remained unsold for over a year, before joining Aeromexico in December 1983 as N3878P, 'Jose Ma. Morelos'. The carrier's ICAO call sign is 'ALITALIA'. *(Author's Collection)*

AMERICAN AIRLINES (AA/AAL)

United States of America

American Airlines was founded in May 1934 as a direct successor to American Airways, formed in 1930, with other predecessor companies dating back to 1926. The carrier has in the past sponsored designs such as the Douglas DC-3, Convair 240, Lockheed 188 Electra, Convair 990, Douglas DC-7 and DC-10. Today, American Airlines is one of the world's largest airlines. It acquired Air Cal in 1986 and absorbed the company in 1987, thus enabling it to provide with a large network of routes along the US West Coast. In 1986 American began the development of five new hubs at Dallas, Chicago, Raleigh/Durham, Nashville and San Juan. An extensive network of feeder routes is operated under the name 'American Eagle', utilizing the services of a number of regional and commuter airlines. The carrier's route structure of scheduled passenger and cargo flights extends from the Atlantic to the Pacific coasts, plus services to Toronto and Montreal in the north, and Mexico City, Acapulco, Guadalajara, Cancun, Cozumel and Puerto Vallarta in the south. In 1971 American absorbed Trans Caribbean Airways, and began flying to Puerto Rico, the US Virgin Islands (as American Inter Island), Aruba, Curaçao and Haiti. The company started services to Bermuda, Barbados and Santo Domingo in 1975 through rights acquired in a route exchange with Pan Am. The carrier also flies to Jamaica and other points in the Caribbean. In May 1982, following the demise of Braniff, American commenced services to London (LGW). It now serves many other cities in Europe, as well as Tokyo (NRT). A fleet of Boeing 727, 737, 747, 757, 767, McDonnell Douglas MD82, 83, British Aerospace 146, Airbus A300, Fokker 100 and Douglas DC-10 types is operated. An order for the MD11 is outstanding to replace its ageing sister, the DC-10. The present livery, although modern in appearance, was actually adopted in 1969. It was designed to take the carrier into the seventies. However, due to the excessive costs in repainting aircraft, it is expected to be around for many years to come. A highly-polished fuselage and tail finish provides a perfect backdrop for a patriotic triple cheatline in red, white and blue. 'American' lettering in red, outlined in white, is displayed on the cabin roof. The tail fin plays host to the traditional company motif of a blue eagle, that swoops down between the peaks of the double 'A' initials. The carrier's ICAO call sign is 'AMERICAN'. *(American Airlines)*

AMERICAN TRANS AIR
(TZ/AMT)

United States of America

American Trans Air was formed in August 1973 by Captain George Mikelsons, to manage the AmbassadAir Travel Club. In March 1981 the company obtained certificates as a common carrier and began offering charter services to the general public, with a number of ex-American Airlines Boeing 707s. Re-equipment plans first began in February 1983, when American Trans Air acquired a DC-10-10. This aircraft, G-BELO, was one of those previously operated by Laker Airways but, because of the collapse of the airline, it had remained out of service for over a year. Having being re-registered N183AT, the new arrival began transatlantic charters for its new owner. In June 1984 it was joined by another of the type, although this time it was one of Northwest Airlines' early Series 40s, and was registered N184AT. Following a change of policy, a whole fleet of ex-Delta Air Lines L-1011 Tristars were taken over in 1985. This led to the sale of N183AT which, following a short period with Air Hawaii, was sold to Cal Air (now Novair International), and became G-GCAL. Its companion, however, survived only a few months longer with American Trans Air, since on August 10, 1986 the DC-10 was destroyed by fire at Chicago. Today the airline, formerly a supplemental (charter) company, is a US certificated air carrier with extensive domestic and international charter operations. It also maintained scheduled passenger services that link Indianapolis with Tampa, Orlando, Fort Myers, Las Vegas and Fort Lauderdale. A line between New York and Bonaire (Netherlands Antilles) is also maintained. An extremely stylish colour scheme features a triple 'straight-through' cheatline in gold, white and blue, separating the grey belly and white cabin roof which displays large 'American Trans Air' titling in dark blue. A cleverly-designed tail motif illustrates a symbolic runway approach using the company's 'ATA' initials in gold and blue, repeated alongside the fuselage on the L-1011 Tristar aircraft only. A fleet of Boeing 727-100, Lockheed L-1011 Tristar Series 1, Series 50 and Grumman G159 Gulfstream 1 aircraft is maintained. Depicted here, on approach to London's Gatwick Airport, is N183AT. The aircraft was operating a flight from Indianapolis. The carrier's ICAO call sign is 'AMTRAN'. *(K. G. Wright)*

ARIANA AFGHAN AIRLINES (FG/AFG)

Afghanistan

Ariana was formed in 1955 by the Afghan Government (51 per cent shareholding), and the Indamer Company of India, the latter having been operating in Afghanistan since the early 1950s. Services commenced with Douglas DC-3s over a domestic network, band to Beirut in 1956. The airline's domestic services were transferred to Bakhtar Afghan Airlines in 1967 so that it could improve links to isolated communities. This enabled Ariana to concentrate on flying Boeing and Douglas types over the 'Marco Polo' route from Kkwaja Rawash Airport, Kabul, to Kandahar (the country's second largest town), Amritsar, Delhi, Tashkent, Istanbul, Moscow (SVO), Paris (ORY), Frankfurt and London (LHR). Charter flights on a regional basis were also provided. In October 1979 a Douglas DC-10-30 (YA-LAS) joined the airline to operate from Kabul to Europe, enabling Ariana to dispose of its Boeing 720 (YA-HBA) in 1980. By 1985 Bakhtar Afghan Airlines took over the operations of the carrier, with that name being adopted. However, by February 1988 it had changed back to its present title. Today, international passenger and cargo services currently link Kabul with Amritsar, Delhi, Dubai, Moscow (SVO), Prague and Tashkent. An extensive domestic network is also operated. Destinations include Bamyan, Chakcharan, Darwaz, Faizabad, Herat, Kabul, Kandahar, Khost, Khwahan, Kunduz, Maimana, Mazar-e-Sharif, Qala-e-Naw, Sheghnan, Tirin and Uruzghan. During the Soviet occupation many flights were disrupted and destinations ceased to be served. This also included the entire European network, and therefore the carrier was forced to dispose of its DC-10; the recipient, in March 1985, was British Caledonian, with whom it was registered G-MULL. Ariana's most attractive royal blue livery was introduced in March 1968 on the airline's first Boeing 727. The current and more colourful scheme replaced the previous livery of a medium blue cheatline or flash carried by the Douglas DC-3s, DC-6s and Convair 440s used by the carrier since its formation in January 1955. First services to London (LGW) were operated by the Douglas DC-6 aircraft, which originally carried a triple 'A' marking on their fins as well as the Ariana stylised bird motif introduced soon after the formation of the company. Jet services were inaugurated with the Boeing 727 early in 1968. The current fleet consists of Boeing 727 (Combis), Antonov AN-24, AN-26, Yakovlev Yak-40 and Tupelov TU-154M types. The airline's ICAO call sign is 'ARIANA'. *(K. G. Wright)*

ARROW AIR (JW/APW) United States of America

Arrow Air was founded in 1947 by George E. Batchelor and was reactivated in 1981. A number of Douglas DC-8s were acquired for long range charters, contract services for the Military Airlift Command, as well as the company's scheduled service between London (LGW) and Florida. Continued growth brought the need for greater capacity on the transatlantic flights, so a pair of Douglas DC-10-10s were leased in 1984. However, increased losses brought cutbacks in operations, thus resulting in the return of these aircraft to their owner. In February 1986 Arrow Air filed for bankruptcy, although it continues in business with a fleet comprising Douglas DC-8-62F (AF) Freighter and Douglas DC-8-63F (CF) Freighter types which are used on cargo flights around the world. Scheduled routes are flown to New York (JFK), Miami, San Juan and Haiti. A base is maintained at the Miami International Airport, Florida. Prior to its bankruptcy, Arrow Air provided scheduled passenger services linking London (LGW), Tampa, Denver, Orlando, Los Angeles, Philadelphia, Boston, Montego Bay, Miami, New York (JFK), San Juan, St. Maarten, Georgetown (Guyana), Toronto and Aruba. A number of hybrid liveries were worn by the Arrow Air fleet, including several actual company identities, although none were ever taken up fleet-wide. The colour scheme displayed here employs the style of the familiar medium blue livery, although some aircraft were painted in red. The broad cheatline runs along the fuselage, below the windows, becoming disjointed as it sweeps up on to the fin and terminates in a huge 'A' initial, encompassing the whole tail from the leading to trailing edges. The overall fuselage colour is white and traditionally-styled 'Arrow Air' titles are carried on the forward fuselage. Seen here on arrival at London's Gatwick Airport is an Arrow Air DC-10, having completed its long flight from Tampa, Florida. The carrier's ICAO call sign is 'BIG A'. *(K. G. Wright)*

BALAIR AG (BB/BBB)   Switzerland

Switzerland's premier charter airline, Balair, was formed in 1953 and began operations the same year as a humble flying school. It was not, however, until 1957 that the company decided to enter the charter market. Today it operates passenger and cargo charters from a base at Basle, in the north of Switzerland, to destinations in the Mediterranean, the Canary Islands, the Far East, North and Central America, East and West Africa, the Middle East and the Caribbean. It is from the name Basle that Balair is derived. Swissair originally held a thirty-six per cent interest in the company, although this has now been increased to fifty-seven per cent. The Swiss charter carrier's modern jet fleet consists of three different types, all of which are common to the parent company, Swissair's, line up. This enables an easy transfer between the fleets to meet demand, when traffic requires. At the present time, Balair operates one example each of the Douglas DC-10-30 (HB-IHK), and an Airbus A-310-322 (ER) (HB-IPK, seating 241). Three McDonnell Douglas MD82s (HB-INB, HB-INR and HB-INW, each of which seat 149) are also maintained, along with a single Fokker F-27 Friendship (seating 34), which is employed exclusively for the United Nations. A

McDonnell Douglas MD83 (HB-ISZ, seating 147) was delivered in April 1990 to supplement the fleet. Balair's sole 345-seat DC-10-30 was delivered on January 31, 1979, and although designed to opérate the carrier's long haul sectors, it has been seen plying the busy IT flights to the Mediterranean and Canaries. The current Balair livery was adopted in 1985, but actually incorporates very few changes from that of the previous scheme. This was the replacement of the black Balair fuselage and tail titles with red, in an identical style, and the removal of the company's somewhat ugly 'B' motif, which had been added only three years earlier. Between these two liveries, a leased MD82 sported a unique title arrangement over its Swissair golden-shadow scheme. This consisted of the 'B' incorporated within the 'Balair' titles but this was never adopted fleetwide. The company chose instead to retain the fresh red cheatline over white of Swissair's earlier style. It should be noted that the tail fin on all types, with the exception of the DC-10, is painted all-red, with a white cross and 'Balair' lettering reversed-out in white at the base. 'Hotel Kilo' is seen just prior to departure from Zurich Airport. The carrier's ICAO call sign is 'BALAIR'. *(K. G. Wright)*

BANGLADESH BIMAN AIRLINES (BG/BBC)

Bangladesh

Bangladesh Biman was formed in January 1972, shortly after the country obtained independence from Pakistan. Scheduled domestic services began the following month, using a sole Douglas DC-3 aircraft. The first intercontinental flight linked the capital city, Dacca, with London (LHR) in March 1972. It was operated with a Boeing 707-331 on wet lease from Tempair International Airlines. This aircraft, S2-ABM, wore Bangladesh Biman titles and the company motif on an all-white fin. In 1983 a total of three Douglas DC-10-30s were purchased from Singapore Airlines. The aircraft are configured to seat a total of 272 people, with the cabins being divided into First, Business, and Economy (Coach) classes. Today, the national flag carrier operates international services to Singapore, Kuala Lumpur, Bangkok, Rangoon, Kathmandu, Calcutta, Bombay, Karachi, Dubai, Abu Dhabi, Kuwait, Muscat, Doha, Dhahran, Jeddah, Tripoli, Athens, Rome, Amsterdam and London (LHR). Domestic services link Dacca with Chittagong, Cox's Bazar, Sylhet, Jessore, Ishurdi, and Saidpur. A relatively modern, western-built fleet of Douglas DC-10, Fokker F-27, and F-28 aircraft is operated. All but

one of the DC-10's were purchased from Singapore Airlines, the other being one of the final aircraft of its type to be built. The current Bangladesh Airlines livery was inspired by the introduction of its first wide-bodied aircraft in 1983. An update of the livery was deemed necessary to reflect a modern international flag, utilizing the national colours of green and red. The company adopted a fashionable white overall finish which effectively modernized the appearance of its ageing Boeing 707s (which are no longer in the fleet), and provided a stylish new look for the DC-10s. The original design has since been slightly revised and now includes horizontal fin bands, which replaced the original vertical cheatline extension. Black titles are carried in English and Bengali on the port and starboard sides respectively. Thus, on the Douglas DC-10, it reads 'Bangladesh Airlines' on the forward upper cabin and 'Biman' on the second engine. Other aircraft types have the livery adapted to suit the fuselage. The motif, representing a white stork flying across a setting sun, is displayed centrally on the fin. The carrier's ICAO call sign is 'BIMAN'. *(K. G. Wright)*

BOGAZICI HAVA TASIMACILIGI/   Turkey
BOSPHORUS AIR TRANSPORT (PQ/BHT)

Bogazici Hava Tasimaciligi was established in December 1986, with operations beginning in July 1987. The company was originally 85 per cent owned by the Turkish national airline, THY. However, all shares in the airline were transferred to the State Housing Development Foundation in 1988 in preparation for privatization. In 1989 the carrier was acquired by a group led by Aer Lingus and Turkish tourism companies for approximately $7.1 million. BHT's main activities are international passenger and cargo charters and scheduled cargo services to Europe and the USA. The only scheduled passenger service provided is from Istanbul to Ankara. It is operated in conjunction with THY, Nesu Air, and Istanbul Airlines. A fleet of Douglas DC-10-10 (seating 345 in all Economy/ Coach), Boeing 707-320C Freighter, and Boeing 727-200 (seating 185 in all Economy/Coach) types is operated. An order is outstanding for two Boeing 737-300 aircraft. The BHT livery consists of a dark blue thin stripe under the window cheatline, with large 'BOGAZICI BHT' titles in the same colour appearing on the forward fuselage. An unusual tail logo of three stripes is seen on the vertical stabilizer, and the Turkish flag sits atop this design. Seen here is TC-JAU 'Jengelky', at Zurich Airport, Switzerland, having operated a charter from Istanbul. This DC-10-10, with construction number 46705, was built in 1972. The aircraft was registered to Douglas as N1338U. It was then delivered to Turk Hava Yollari — Turkish Airlines, on December 1, 1972. From there it saw nearly fourteen years of worldwide service with the Turkish national airline, before being stored at Istanbul for several months. In December of that year, this aircraft, along with its sistership, TC-JAY 'Yenikoy', was transferred to Bosphorus Air Transport, although the latter has since been returned to THY. Two Boeing 707-321Cs were also delivered from THY these being TC-JCC 'Uskudar', and TC-JCF 'Beylerbeyl'. Two Boeing 727-264s are leased-in from Aeron Aviation. TC-JFA 'Ortakoy' was originally Mexican registered as XA-TAC, whilst TC-JFB 'Vanikoy' was previously XA-TAB. The carrier's ICAO call sign is 'BASFIR'. *(K. G. Wright)*

BRITISH AIRWAYS PLC (BA/BAW)

United Kingdom

British Airways was formed in September 1972 through the merger of British Overseas Airways Corporation (founded in 1940), British European Airways (founded in 1946), and British Air Services. Formally integrated operations began on April 1, 1974, and the airline was further rationalized into a single unified operation structure in April 1977. A little under ten years later, in February 1987, the carrier was privatized. The sale of 720 million shares raised £900 million, attracted 1.1 million small investors, and was 11 times oversubscribed. British Airways carries the most international passenger traffic of any of the world's airlines and is the UK's national carrier. During 1988 the company was allowed to complete the integration of British Caledonian Airways, which it had acquired in December 1987. The airline's worldwide scheduled service route network covers over 165 destinations in nearly 80 countries. These include the UK and Europe, the Near, Middle and Far East, Australasia, Africa, the Caribbean, and North and South America. Domestic services, which link over 15 points in the UK, include the carrier's 'Shuttle' (high frequency, no reservations, guaranteed seat) services between London (LHR) and Belfast, Edinburgh, Glasgow and Manchester. In 1989, due to increased competition from British Midland (from LHR), and Air UK (from LGW), on these routes,

British Airways decided to revamp its service. Now called 'Super Shuttle', the carrier still operates a high frequency service but, in addition to advance reservations, it also offers meals at all times of the day. During the 1988/9 financial year, British Airways began, and in some cases, reopened, services to Ankara, Baghdad, Madras, Malmo, San Diego, Seoul, and Tehran. At the same time the airline ceased flights to Casablanca, Tunis and Malta due to poor load factors. Subsidiary companies include Caledonian Airways, the carrier's charter arm, which operates inclusive-tour services from its base at London (LGW), and from other UK airports. British Airways' fleet consists of BAe Concorde, 748, 1-11, ATP, Boeing 737, 747, 757, 767, L-1011 Tristar, and Airbus A320 types. During 1989, the carrier temporarily leased-in two BAe 146 aircraft from Presidential Airlines, due to lack of aircraft availability. An order for several McDonnell Douglas MD-11 types, which had been inherited from the BCAL merger, were sold to American Airlines before the aircraft had even been built. Seen here at Houston is Douglas DC-10-30, G-NIUK. The carrier's ICAO call sign is 'SPEEDBIRD', although when aircraft are operating the shuttle, the call sign used is 'SHUTTLE'. *(K. G. Wright)*

BRITISH CALEDONIAN AIRWAYS (BR/BCA)

United Kingdom

British Caledonian was formed on November 30, 1970, when charter carrier, Caledonian Airways, took over British United Airways. After two years of operating under the name of Caledonian/BUA, the company was renamed British Caledonian Airways. Following a change in government policy for civil aviation in 1976, the airline became the sole British flag carrier to Central and West Africa and South America. It became necessary to evaluate wide-bodied aircraft, and to that end, the DC-10 was chosen. This resulted in an order for two DC-10-30s to cover the long haul sectors. In the mid-1980s, charters and scheduled services were flown on behalf of Caribbean Airways, between the West Indies and Brussels, Air Seychelles between Mahe, Frankfurt and London (LGW), together with trips for Surinam Airways. Two secondhand DC-10-30s were acquired in 1985, these coming from Ariana Afghan Airlines and Air Zaire. In December 1987, British Airways acquired the carrier, with final integration taking place in the following year. Prior to this, BCAL was the second largest UK carrier, and always posed a threat to the national airline. It flew scheduled passenger services throughout the United Kingdom and to points in Europe, North America, Africa, the Middle and Far East. Prior to its take-over, its fleet consisted of Douglas DC-10, BAe 1-11, Boeing 747 and Airbus Industrie A310 aircraft. An order for seven airbus A320s was later taken over by British Airways, although the order for a quantity of MD11 types was not. The delivery positions of these were sold to American Airlines before delivery. British Caledonian had a distinctive livery, the highlight being a rampant heraldic lion. This dominated the entire tail fin on a deep blue background. A dark blue cheatline above a similar band in gold, separated the white and grey lower fuselage. Black 'British Caledonian' lettering was followed by the Union Flag on both sides of the fuselage, with the coloquial 'BCAL' logo and shield appearing on the engines of the A310s and DC10s only. A Scottish flavour was maintained through the use of tartan uniforms and aircraft names, alongside small Scottish flags. The carrier's ICAO call sign was 'CALEDONIAN'.
(K. G. Wright)

CANADIAN AIRLINES INTERNATIONAL (CP/CDN)

Canada

Canadian Airlines International is the name of the two merged carriers. Canadian Pacific and Pacific Western Airlines. The merger, which took place in April 1987, became legally effective on January 1, 1988. Prior to this, Canadian Pacific was Canada's second-largest airline, operating a large network of international and domestic routes, whilst PWA was one of the country's biggest regional carriers. The new company is fully owned by PWA Corporation, which is a widely held Canadian airline with no one shareholder able to own more than four per cent of the outstanding common stock. Canadian Pacific was formed in 1942 when the railway company of this name acquired and amalgamated ten bush operators. Initially the airline maintained services in North West and Western Canada, but international services began in 1949. Eastern Provincial Airways was acquired in 1984, together with its affiliate, Air Maritime. In 1985 Nordair was acquired, and it was amalgamated into CP on January 2, 1987. The airline gained control of Quebecair in 1986 (through its subsidiary Nordair Metro) and, later that year, took a 35 per cent stake in Air Atlantic. Pacific Western Airlines was founded in 1946 as Central British Columbia Airlines and adopted the name PWA In 1953. In 1970 the carrier took over BC Airlines,

and in May 1977 it acquired a 72 per cent holding in Transair of Winnipeg. The official merger between PWA and Transair took place in 1979, with operations integrated under the PWA name. Today, Canadian Pacific operates a fleet of Douglas DC-10, Boeing 737, 747, 767, Fairchild FH227, Lockheed L-188 Electra and BAe 748 aircraft. The airline operates international services to Amersterdam, Lisbon, Milan, Buenos Aires, Lima. Rio de Janeiro, Santiago, Sao Paulo, Bangkok, Beijing, Hong Kong, Shanghai, Tokyo (NRT), Aukland, Sydney, Nadi, Honolulu, Los Angeles and San Francisco. An extensive network of domestic and trans-border services to around eighty destinations is all operated. The carrier has formed the largest network of commuter services in Canada, operating under the 'Canadian Partner' logo. Carriers participating under this alliance include Air Atlantic, Calm Air, Ontario Express, Norcan Air, and Time Air. PWA Corporation has a minority interest in each 'Canadian Partner'. In 1989, Canadian Airlines International purchased Wardair, and all aircraft and services were integrated by 1990. Seen here is Douglas DC-10-30, C-GCFI, on October 7, 1987, on arrival at Hong Kong's Kai Tak Airport. The carrier's ICAO call sign is 'EMPRESS'. *(B. J. Eagles)*

CANADIAN PACIFIC AIR LINES (CP)   Canada

Originally known as Canadian Pacific Airlines, from 1968 the airline adopted the shorter and more recognisable title of CP Air. However, in 1986 the carrier reverted to its previous name in an effort to obtain a new company image. International routes were begun in 1949 with particular emphasis on those across the Pacific. When the wide-bodied era arrived, CP Air became a Boeing 747 operator some years before its first DC-10-30 arrived in 1979. Both types were subsequently to be used on transatlantic charters, as well as on the company's scheduled service to Amsterdam. During 1983, CP Air found, to its advantage, that a deal could be made with United Air Lines. In this it could exchange three of its long range models for an equal number of Series 10s. At the time of this agreement, the Canadian company had decided to reduce its involvement in IT work. However, these relative newcomers became frequent travellers across the Atlantic thereafter. By the beginning of 1986, CP Air was in possession of eight Series 30s. At this stage the company decided that it would standardize on the type by exchanging its four Boeing 747s for a similar number of DC-10s belonging to Pakistan International. However, hardly had they been delivered, when it was announced in the autumn that that airline had been taken over by Pacific Western, and that the combined fleet was to operate under the banner of Canadian Airlines International, from 1987 (see separate entry). *(K. G. Wright)*

CONDOR FLUNGDIENST (DF/CFG)

Federal Republic of Germany

Condor was formed in October 1961 by the merger of Deutsche Flugdienst (founded in 1958 as a Lufthansa subsidiary) and Condor Luftreederei (founded in 1957 and acquired by Lufthansa in 1959). Today the company is regarded as one of the world's largest charter airlines, operating intercontinental tour and general passenger group flights with an all-jet fleet of aircraft. Regular tour charter services are operated from Frankfurt, Dusseldorf, Munich and Stuttgart. Other German gateways include Hamburg, Bremen, Hannover and Saarbrucken. Condor operates package tour flights to destinations in Spain, Greece, the Canary Islands, Italy, Portugal, Turkey, Tunisia, Morocco, Kenya, Thailand, Sri Lanka, the United States, Canada, and Mexico. An emphasis is given to a very high quality of service, which the airline prides itself upon. A fleet of Douglas DC-10, Airbus Industrie A310 and Boeing 727 types are operated. The Boeing 737-300 and Boeing 757-200 equipment owned by Condor are in fact operated by DFD Deutsche Ferien-

flugdienste (a division of Condor, with the same headquarters), and Sudflug Suddeutsche Flugges, respectively. The airline's livery was originally deisgned with tasteful practicality in mind. Unfortunately, however, a design change was necessary following the delivery of the company's first Airbus A310. This was done through the re-painting of the otherwise natural metal fuselage to a distinctive overall pale grey, which has now been adopted fleetwide. A lemon yellow fin adds the neccessary touch of colour and displays a styled encircled flying Condor bird motif in a deep blue. This has been repeated under the cockpit windows and on each engine cowling, which is complemented by bold 'Condor' titles in a deep blue, near the forward passenger door. It should be noted that the Boeing 737s and 757s wear the full Condor livery, but with the DFD or Sudflug titles. Seen here on October 23, 1986, at Frankfurt Airport, is a DC-10-30 operated in Condor's original 'bare metal' livery. The carrier's ICAO call sign is 'CONDOR'. *(B. T. Richards)*

CONTINENTAL AIRLINES (CO/COA)

United States of America

Continental's formation dates from July 15, 1934, when it began services as Varney Speed Lines. In May 1937 Varney purchased the Denver-Pueblo route of Wyoming Air Service and moved its headquarters to Denver. Later the same year the name Continental Airlines was adopted. Development continued for a number of years until the 1955 award of the Chicago-Los Angeles route (via Kansas City and Denver) marked the company's full transition to a mainline trunk carrier. In October 1981 Texas Air, parent company of Texas International Airlines, acquired a controlling interest in Continental, and on October 31, 1982, after several months of operating co-ordinated schedules, the airline, along with Texas International, started to operate as a single carrier, under the name Continental. Texas International, known until 1969 as Trans-Texas Airways, and formed originally in 1940 as Aviation Enterprises, commenced scheduled services in October 1947. In September 1983, Continental filed for protection under Chapter 11, and as a result the company's domestic network was reduced from 78 points to 25 and its workforce declined from 12,000 to 4,200. Since then the company's financial position has improved dramatically, and by the end of 1984 the airline was already offering more capacity than before its Chapter 11 filing. In September 1985 Continental filed a plan of reorganization with the US Bankruptcy Court and a year later emerged from Chapter 11 protection. In February 1987 the operations of the People Express Group (Frontier, People Express, Britt Airways, and Provincetown Boston Airlines) and New York Air were merged into the carrier. Continental operates an extensive network of scheduled passenger services, covering 82 US domestic and 42 international destinations. The airline has four major traffic hubs at Denver, Houston, New York (EWR), and Cleveland. Its international network serves Australia, New Zealand, United Kingdom, France, Mexico, Canada, Japan, Micronesia, and Tahiti. The airline operates an extensive network of domestic feeder services under the name 'Continental Express'. These are provided by the following carriers: Britt Airways, Bar Harbour Airlines, Rocky Mountain Airways, and Southern Jersey Airways. A fleet of Douglas DC-10, DC-9, McDonnell Douglas MD80, Airbus Industrie A300, Boeing, 727, 737 and 747 aircraft is maintained. The carrier's ICAO sign is 'CONTINENTAL'. *(K. G. Wright)*

DELTA AIR LINES (DL/DAL)

United States of America

Delta Air Lines was founded in 1924 as the world's first crop-dusting company, and began passenger services in 1929. In 1953 the airline merged with Chicago and Southern Airlines (founded in 1933), and in 1972 it absorbed Northeast Airlines (also founded in 1933). When the 1968 battle for orders was underway, Delta was one of the major carriers to support the Lockheed L-1011 Tristar in preference to the Douglas DC-10. However, having ordered the former type, the airline took out an insurance policy against possible late delivery by ordering five DC-10-10s on March 18, 1971. Following negotiations, Delta sold the five aircraft to United Airlines, but immediately leased them back for two-and-a-half-years, when it was anticipated that the carrier would have a sufficient number of L-1011's to be on strength. DC-10s N601DA–N605DA served on transcontinental routes until the Spring of 1975 when they were delivered to United as N1833U–N1837U respectively. The Atlanta-based airline absorbed Western Airlines in April 1987 to form the then third largest US carrier. Today, Delta operates from five major hubs at Atlanta, Cincinnati, Dallas/Fort Worth, Salt Lake City, and Los Angeles, with services provided throughout the USA to over 160 locations. International destinations include those in Canada, Europe, and the Far East. An extensive feeder network is operated under the 'Delta Connection' banner. This involves four commuter airlines: Comair (Cincinnati/Orlando), Business Express (New York/Boston), Atlantic Southeast (Atlanta/Dallas), and Sky West (Salt Lake City/Los Angeles). Delta's company name was originally taken from the Mississipi Delta and is illustrated by a large blue and red delta on the fin and on the fuselage behind the cockpit. This scheme is affectionately known as the 'widget'. The dark blue windowline is separated from the 'Delta' fuselage titling by a full length narrow red pinstripe, and at a point in line with the cockpit windows this subtly merges with the black extended anti-dazzle panel. Although the lower fuselage is now left in natural metal, a broad band of white follows the contour of the cheatline down to wing level. A fleet of Douglas DC-9, L-1011 Tristar, Boeing 737, 757, 767, McDonnell Douglas MD82, and MD88 types are operated. Outstanding orders for quantities of the MD11 and MD90 will see delivery in the 'nineties. Seen at Honolulu is a Delta DC-10-10, as purchased from Western Airlines. This particular aircraft, along with the rest of the DC-10s that were operated by the latter company, are no longer with Delta. The carrier's ICAO call sign is 'DELTA'. *(B. T. Richards)*

EASTERN AIR LINES (EA/EAL)

United States of America

Eastern Airlines was formed in 1926 as Pitcairn Aviation, starting a mail service between New York and Atlanta in May 1928. In the following year the company was acquired by North American Aviation, the name being changed to Eastern Air Transport. In 1938 North American relinquished its holdings and the company adopted the present title after some reorganization. Several other airlines have been absorbed, including New York Airways (1931), Ludington Airlines (1933), Colonial Airways (1956), Mackey Airlines (1967), and Caribbean Atlantic Airlines (1974). On January 1, 1983, Eastern became the first airline to put the Boeing 757 into service. Following the demise of Air Florida, the carrier was awarded the Miami-London (LGW) route in 1984, and transatlantic operations began on July 15 of the following year. With only one of the three ordered ex-Alitalia DC-10s on strength, only a three times weekly schedule was maintained at first, although this was increased to daily as the fleet increased in size. Load factors were high during the first few months of operation, but gradually there was a steady decline. This was partly due to the reluctance at the time of US citizens to visit Europe. However, one of the main reasons was that Eastern blamed Virgin Atlantic for its introduction of a competitive fare structure. Whatever the real reason, Eastern was not prepared to continue a loss-making route on an indefinite basis, and it was therefore announced in early August 1986 that the airline would withdraw from the service at the end of October. That same month, Eastern was acquired by Frank Lorenzo's Texas Air Corporation. On March 9, 1989, due to ever decreasing passenger loads, the carrier filed for Chapter 11 bankruptcy. In the previous year it had considerably reduced the scale of its operations; its traffic levels for December 1988 were 20 per cent down on the same month a year earlier. Eastern pulled out of several routes in September of that year, in a drastic attempt to improve its financial position. This involved the closure of its Kansas City hub, and overall had the effect of reducing staff by 4,000, and capacity by over 10 per cent. The following month it announced the sale of its profitable shuttle operation to Donald Trump. Major disagreements between the airline's management and its unionized workforce have been associated with each of these cutbacks. Despite its bankruptcy, Eastern is operating a small number of services to places in mainland USA. Prior to this, the airline operated to destinations in the US, Canada, the Caribbean, and South America. Feeder services were organized and operated under the name 'Eastern Express'. Eastern's livery has basically remained unchanged since the current image of a 'great silver fleet' was introduced in 1977. Twin cheatlines in light and dark blue, or 'Caribbean' and 'Ionosphere' as they are known to Eastern, sweep along the fuselage and up to the tail, parallel with its leading edge. Simple dark blue 'Eastern' fuselage lettering, outlined in white, accompanies the styled Falcon motif and national flag on the cabin roof. A fleet of Douglas DC-10, DC-9, Boeing 727, 757, Airbus A300 and L-1011 Tristar equipment was operated, prior to the collapse of what was one of the USA's largest carriers. Seen here in July 1988 is one of the ex-Alitalia DC-10-30s. The aircraft is depicted at Los Angeles International Airport, and was being prepared for a flight to Miami, Florida. The airline's ICAO call sign is 'EASTERN'.

(B. T. Richards)

ECUATORIANA (EU/EEA)   Ecuador

Ecuatoriana was formed in July 1974 as the national airline of Ecuador and took over the operating rights, debts and assets of the private airline Compania Ecuatoriana de Aviacion (CEA), itself formed in May 1957. The Government of Ecuador gained limited control of the carrier in 1972, and full control in July 1974. The airline acquired its first wide-bodied type from Swissair in August 1983. As HB-IHA, it was the European airline's first DC-10 to arrive in Zurich, back in November 1972. When it arrived in Eduador it was re-registered HC-BKO. It has subsequently been employed on the carrier's schedules linking Quito and Guayquil with Los Angeles, Miami, New York (JFK) and Panama. Today, the company operates scheduled passenger services from Quito and Guayaquil to New York (JFK), Los Angeles, Chicago, Caracas, Santiago, Panama City, Cali, Lima, Mexico City, Bogota, San Jose, and Buenos Aires, and an all-cargo service to Miami, Panama City and New York (JFK). Engineering and technical support is provided under contract by Israel Aircraft Industries. A fleet of Douglas DC-10 and Boeing 707

types is maintained. Although a significant departure from the flamboyant Indian style schemes of the seventies, the current Ecuatoriana livery is widely regarded as one of the world's most attractive, promoting a stylish and distinctive company image. An all-cream fuselage forms the backdrop for six bands of bright colour, yellow, green, and blue sweeping down from the cabin roof and magenta, orange, and red rising from the fuselage undersides. The resulting six-part cheatline continues along the rear of the fuselage and flows up on to the tail, where it is surmounted by the company's traditional 'E' motif in black and white. The entire passenger fleet of Boeing 707s, and the DC-10, now wear this standard livery, but the 707 freighter, HC-BGP, sports a unique gold fuselage-finish, standard six-part cheatlines and additional 'Ecuatoriana Jet Cargo' titling and freight motif in black. Seen here at Zurich is HC-BKO, prior to its delivery. Note the hybrid livery of a basic Swissair cheatline, but with Ecuatoriana titling and tail logo. The carrier's ICAO call sign is 'ECUATORIANA'. *(K. G. Wright)*

FEDERAL EXPRESS CORPORATION (MB/FDX)

United States of America

Federal Express was formed in 1971 by the current chairman and CEO, Frederick W. Smith. Operations began in 1973 using Falcon 20 business jets. Following CAB deregulation of air cargo in November 1977, authority to operate larger aircraft was received, and a fleet of Boeing 727, 737 and Douglas DC-10 aircraft was progressively assembled. Today, Federal Express is a 'hub-and-spoke' all-freight carrier. It specializes in door-to-door express delivery of packages and documents. The centre of operations is the company's facility at Memphis International Airport, from which an extensive network of nightly cargo services is operated to every major market throughout the USA (including Alaska). Brussels (which is the sorting centre for the European market), and London (STN) have been included in the network since 1986. Toronto and Montreal are also served. Mini-hubs are operated at Newark and Oakland. The company's worldwide service network covers approximately 85 countries, either directly of through contracted agents. Documents and packages not exceeding 150 lb or 130 inches in length and girth combined are carried. The services offered include 'Overnight Letter' and 'Priority One' (delivery no later than the second working day), 'Courier Pak' and 'ZapMail' (a facsimile document transmission service, now available also to the major European cities, Hong Kong, and throughout the UK). The company purchased Lex Wilkinson, a British package and delivery company, in January 1986, for future expansion into the UK. In 1989, the Flying Tiger Line was purchased by the carrier to enlarge its network of services and to increase the company's fleet, the former airline's infantry consisting of Douglas DC-8 and Boeing 747 types. Today, Federal Express maintains a fleet of aircraft that includes the Douglas DC-10, Boeing 727 and Canadair CL-600. Operation of the company's huge fleet of Cessna Caravans is contracted out to Baron Aviation, Corporate Air, Mountain Air Cargo, PM Air, Union Flights and Wiggins Airways. On order is a quantity of McDonnell Douglas MD11 aircraft, to increase capacity. Federal Express was the first carrier to order the cargo variant of this aircraft. The carrier's ICAO call sign is 'FEDEX'. *(B. J. Eagles)*

FINNAIR O/Y (AY/FIN)   Finland

Finnair, known until 1968 as Aero, was founded in November 1923, and began operations in March of the following year. Seaplanes were used exclusively until 1936, when the first airports were built in Finland. Originally a private company, the Government now has a 76.1 per cent holding. Finland's national carrier celebrated its 65th anniversary on November 1, 1988. The company operates an extensive network of international scheduled services from Helsinki. In all, 35 destinations are served, mainly in Europe. Long haul flights are operated to Bangkok, Singapore, Tokyo (NRT) and Beijing in the Far East, and to Los Angeles, Montreal, New York (JFK) and Seattle in North America. A new service to Toronto was inaugurated in April 1989, and is currently the only non-stop service between any of the Nordic countries and this Canadian city. The non-stop Helsinki to Beijing service, which began in June 1988, provides the fastest connection between Europe and the People's Republic of China, with an average eight hour flight time. Finnair also operates one of the world's densest domestic networks relative to the population, serving a 22-point system within the country. Wholly owned subsidiaries include Area Travel Agency, Finntours (tour operations), Finncharter (Canada), Nordic-Hotel, Finncatering, and Aero (holding company). Finnair also has holdings in Finnaviation (90 per cent), and Karair (35.1 per cent), Finland Travel Bureau (99 per cent), United Travel (81.1 per cent), Mikkelin Matkaoimisto (51 per cent) (travel agency), and Sunntours Ltd (96.6 per cent). A fleet of Douglas DC-9-40, -50, DC-10, MD-82, -83, -87, Airbus A300, ATR 42 and 72 aircraft are operated. As well as these, a Boeing 737-210C (from Express One), is leased-in, although as a freighter, and the aircraft is operated by Atlanta Icelandic, on behalf of Finnair. An order for the McDonnell Douglas MD-11 is outstanding. Finnair's light, bright and clean cut livery of blue and white is based upon the national colours of the Finnish flag. The motif is a stylized 'F', for Finnair, inset in a blue circle. It was designed by a Mr Kyosti Waris, and first introduced in 1960. Depicted here is one of the airline's five DC-10-30's. The carrier's ICAO call sign is 'FINNAIR'. *(K. G. Wright)*

GARUDA INDONESIA (GA/GIA)   Indonesia

Garuda Indonesia, formerly known as Garuda Indonesian Airways, is the state-owned Indonesian national airline. Scheduled passenger and cargo services are operated from Jakarta to London (LGW), Amsterdam, Frankfurt, Paris (ORY), Abu Dhabi, Jeddah, Colombo, Bangkok, Kuala Lumpur, Penang, Singapore, Hong Kong, Manila, Sydney, Perth, Melbourne, and to Tokyo (NRT) via Denpasar. Garuda's domestic network extends one-tenth of the way round the world, linking Jakarta with more than thirty points throughout the archipelago. The company was formed on March 31, 1950 by the Indonesian Government and KLM, as the successor to the post-war Inter-Island Division of KLM and the pre-war KNILM. Nationalization took over De Kkroonduif's domestic operations in West New Guinea, but a year later they were handed over to PT Merpati Nursantara, the nationalized domestic operator. Garuda took over Merpati in October 1978. Subsidiary companies include Merpati-Nursantara Airlines, the Sanur Beach and Nusa Dua Beach hotels, the catering subsidiary PT Angkasa Citra Sarana, and Satriavi Travel Service. A fleet of Douglas DC-10, DC-9, Fokker 100, F-28, Airbus A300 and Boeing 737 aircraft is operated, An order for the McDonnell Douglas MD11 and Airbus A330 has been placed for delivery during the 'nineties. The current Garuda livery was unveiled in September 1985, when a Douglas DC-10 was repainted to coincide with the Indonesian President's European visit. Designed by Walter Landor & Associates of San Francisco, the dramatic new image centres on a bird motif, consisting of five stripes to represent the five national ideals, which appear in various shades of light-blue and turquoise. These get progressively greener from nose to tail, and are displayed on the all-dark blue fin alongside the new-style 'Garuda Indonesia' titles, also in dark blue. A pure white fuselage finish contrasts smartly with the blue tail and titles, thus giving the livery a modern and fashionable feel. It should be noted that the Indonesian flag appears alongside the forward passenger door. Douglas DC-10-30, PK-GIA, is seen here on October 7, 1987, whilst on approach to Hong Kong's Kai Tak International Airport. The carrier's ICAO call sign is 'INDONESIA'. *(B. J. Eagles)*

GHANA AIRWAYS CORPORATION (GA/GHA)

Ghana

Ghana Airways was formed in July 1958 by the Ghanaian Government and BOAC, to take over the Ghana operations of the former West African Airways Corporation. Flight operations began on July 16 of that year, over an Accra-London (LHR) route. The Government secured full ownership of the airline in 1961. Today the carrier maintains international scheduled passenger and cargo services to Europe, serving Dusseldorf, London (LHR), and Rome, and regional flights in West Africa, linking Accra with Abidjan, Banjul, Conakry, Cotonou, Dakar, Freetown, Lomé, and Monrovia. The company also operates domestic scheduled services that link the capital with Kumasi, Sunyani, and Tamale. A single example each of the Douglas DC-10-30, DC-9-51, Fokker F-28-2000 and F-28-4000 types are maintained. The Ghana Airways livery is based upon the Ghanaian national colours of red, yellow and green, incorporating within the motif, the national black five-pointed star. The emblem is carried on the centre engine on the DC-10, surmounted by a large representa-

tion of the flag and repeated on other engines. Fuselage titles appear in the black of the national star and are accompanied by a further flag. The Fokker Fellowships and DC-9-51 wear an all-white fuselage with a Ghanaian tail flag and standard fuselage lettering. The livery was in fact introduced in late 1974. Prior to this date, the aircraft sported a light blue cheatline with Ghana Airways titling in red. When the carrier was in possession of its Vickers VC-10, the aircraft was painted in this scheme, with the addition of the main passenger doors being painted in yellow, with the logo appearing in its centre. Since Ghana Airways does not employ its DC-10 on a very rigorous schedule, the aircraft can often be seen operating services for other carriers. Seen here is the sole Ghanaian registered widebodied aircraft, a DC-10-30, 9G-ANA. It is depicted here, at London's Heathrow Airport, whilst taxiing to runway 27R, for departure on the company's non-stop flight, GH701, to Accra. ICAO call sign for the carrier is 'GHANA'. *(Aviation Photo News)*

IBERIA (IB/IBE) Spain

Iberia was founded in 1940 as Lineas Aereas de España, from a succession of carriers dating back to 1921. It progressively modernized its long haul fleet from 1968, when the first DC-8-63 was delivered. The DC-10s were primarily used on medium density routes to North, Central and South America, the Middle East and Africa. Gradually, more and more of the type were delivered to Iberia, until in June 1980 the number in service reached eight, with the arrival of EC-DHZ. The airline is state owned and is controlled through the Instituto Nacional de Industria. This was followed, in 1970, by the Boeing 747. At present, the national carrier of Spain is being substantially reorganized to create a number of clearly defined profit centres, clearing the way for partial privatization. Iberia has recently established a subsidiary airline, Binter Canarias, to operate scheduled passenger services in the Canary Islands, which is currently provided by Aviaco. A fleet of CASA/IPTN CN235 aircraft is maintained by Binter, and this was supplemented by ATR 72 types in the latter part of 1989. Iberia also plans a similar venture in the Balearic Islands. It is also a major shareholder in Viva (48 per cent), a charter carrier, jointly owned with Lufthansa. Other subsidiaries include Binter Mediterranean and Binter Cantabrica. The Spanish airline operates a large network of scheduled passenger and cargo services in North, Central and South America, Africa, Europe, the Middle and Far East. An extensive domestic network is also provided. A fleet of Douglas DC-10, DC-9, MD-87, Boeing 727, 747, and Airbus A300 aircraft is maintained. As well as these types, several examples of the Boeing 737-300 and McDonnell Douglas MD 83 are owned, although they are operated by other carriers, Outstanding orders for Airbus A320 and A340 aircraft are awaited. Delivery of the first type begins in October 1990, with the rest following throughout the decade. Seen here is Douglas DC-10-30, EC-CLB, whilst on approach to London's Heathrow Airport. 'Costa Blanca' made an unexpected visit to the UK, since flights from Madrid are normally operated by Airbus A300. Douglas DC-9 or Boeing 727 aircraft. The carrier's ICAO call sign is 'IBERIA'. *(K. G. Wright)*

JAPAN AIR LINES (JL/JAL)   Japan

Japan Air Lines is the successor to the original privately owned company of the same name, which began operating in August 1951. The new JAL came into being in October 1953 as the national airline with a Government holding of fifty per cent. Today, JAL is a fully privately owned company, with 52,893 shareholders, the Japanese Government having sold its 34.5 per cent stake in the carrier in 1987. In 1986, JAL lost its monopoly of scheduled international passenger services when All Nippon Airways began operations to Guam, Los Angeles and Washington (IAD). However, JAL was able to launch its first new domestic services since 1972, linking Tokyo (HND) with Fukuoka. In April 1986 the airline initiated nonstop Tokyo (NRT)-London (LHR) and Tokyo (NRT)-Paris (CDG) flights. The company is the largest operator of Boeing 747 aircraft, having used at one time or another all variants, with the exception of the 'SP'. One version that JAL currently operates, the 300SR, seats 563 passengers. The Japanese national flag carrier operates an extensive network of scheduled passengers and cargo services, covering 59 cities in 34 countries. Services link Tokyo (NRT), Osaka, Naha, Sapporo, Fukuoka, Kagoshima, and Nagoya with numerous points in Asia and the Middle East, Australia (Sydney), New Zealand (Aukland), North America (Anchorage, Vancouver, Seattle, Atlanta, San Francisco, Los Angeles, Chicago and New York (JFK)), Central America (Mexico City), South America (Rio de Janeiro), and Europe (London (LHR), Paris (CDG), Amsterdam, Dusseldorf, Copenhagen, Hamburg, Frankfurt, Zurich, Rome, Athens, and Madrid), and Moscow. Subsidiary companies include Japan Asia Airways (100 per cent), Southwest Airlines (51 per cent), Japan Air Lines Development Company (76 per cent), Airport Ground Service (87.5 per cent), Nikko Trading Co. (70 per cent), and Japan Creative Tours (50 per cent). A fleet of Boeing 747, 767, and Douglas DC-10 types is maintained. Although the previous company livery is depicted here, the current scheme was introduced in 1989 to coincide with a new corporate image. The tail emblem still consists of the 'Tsuru', a large rising sun formed by outstretched wings of a red crane with white 'JAL' lettering. The fuselage is now white, with a stylized large 'JAL' appearing on the forward section of the aircraft. Small 'Japan Airlines' titles are situated just before the company name. A colour 'flash' cheatline is added on the forward fuselage. The grey undersides have been kept from the previous livery. The carrier's ICAO call sign is 'JAPANAIR'. *(Japan Air Lines)*

J.A.T. — JUGOSLOVENSKI AEROTRANSPORT (JU/JAT)

Yugoslavia

JAT was founded on April 1, 1947, by the Yugoslav Government. Its aim was to take over from the Yugoslav Air Force the operations of domestic and international passenger services, utilizing two Junkers Ju-52s and two Douglas DC-3 aircraft. Today, the state-owned flag carrier operates scheduled services to all major European destinations, as well as to cities in North America, the Middle and Far East, Africa and Australia. In addition to this, a comprehensive domestic network is maintained. Air Jugoslavia is a subsidiary formed to operate charters, using JAT equipment when required. JAT undertakes maintenance for its own aircraft, as well as for other airlines. The Yugoslavian carrier also operates the following: Airlift (tour operator), JAT Catering, JAT Training Centre, JAT Medical Centre, Agricultural Aviation, two airports, and JAT ground transportation. A fleet of Douglas DC-10, DC-9, Boeing 707, 727, 737, aircraft is maintained. Examples of the ATR-72 and McDonnell Douglas MD11 are currently on order, pending delivery within the next two years. The latter type will replace its olders sisters on the Yugoslavian carrier's long haul routes to the USA, Middle and Far East and Australia. As with many national airlines, the colours of the country's flag are widely used. On this occasion it provides the blue and red of the cheatlines. The starboard fuselage features English 'Yugoslav Airlines' titling, with 'Jugoslovenski Aerotransport' appearing on the port. The red and white traditional 'JAT' logo has remained unchanged and is displayed boldly on the predominantly blue fin. A brand new livery was introduced during August 1985 to coincide with the delivery of the carrier's first Boeing 737-300. It features a highly polished natural metal fuselage, together with a more modern below-the-window cheatline arrangement. The DC-10s, however, retain the old livery of a blue window level cheatline with a red pinstripe beneath. Red 'Jugoslovenski Aerotransport' titles appear on the forward fuselage, with the Jugoslavian flag at the rear of the aircraft. A dark blue covers the tail fin, with the 'JAT' motif appearing in the centre. This livery is in fact worn by all of the fleet with, of course, the exception of the Boeing 737-300 aircraft. One of the Yugoslav registered Douglas DC-10-30s can be seen here, just prior to its delivery to Belgrade. The airline's ICAO call sign is 'JAT'.
(K. G. Wright)

KLM — ROYAL DUTCH AIRLINES (KL/KLM)

Netherlands

KLM, the national carrier of the Netherlands, is now the world's oldest operating airline. The airline is able to trace its history back to October 7, 1919. Its initial service was between Amsterdam and London in 1920, with a two-passenger de Havilland DH 16. A European network was subsequently formed, followed in 1929 by an extension to Java. Operations were begun in the West Indies in 1935, and these were continued throughout the Second World War, thus enabling KLM to claim more than 65 years of continuous operation. In 1986 the Dutch Government reduced its holding in the company to 39.4 per cent through the sale of three million shares. KLM is a member of KSSU, a consortium with SAS, Swissair, and UTA, which provides for the joint maintenance of the companies' widebodied aircraft. The airline currently operates a network of scheduled passenger and cargo services from its base at Amsterdam's Schipol Airport to 129 cities in 79 countries, spread throughout Europe; North, Central and South America; Africa; the Near, Middle and Far East; and Australia. A fleet of Douglas DC-10, DC-9, Boeing 737, 747, and Airbus Industrie A310 types is operated. KLM was one of the first European carriers to take delivery of the Boeing 747-400 aircraft, when the first of the type for the carrier, PH-BFA, was delivered in 1989. Wholly owned subsidiaries include KLM Aerocarto, KLM Helicopters, Netherlines and NLM City Hopper. Stakes are held in Martinair, Schreiner Aviation, XP Express Parcel Systems and Air UK. The two tones of blue that appear in today's KLM livery have been used for well over thirty years in various forms. A deep blue windowline is flanked by a bold white stripe below, and an all-light blue cabin roof above, displaying reversed out white registration and fuselage logo. The latter appearing in a comparatively small form. The fin is all white and promotes the company logo, which consists of dark blue 'KLM' letters, topped by a light blue stylized crown, to emphasise the 'Royal' Dutch Airlines. Seen here is PH-DTF, a Douglas DC-10-30. The carrier's ICAO call sign is 'KLM'.
(KLM — Royal Dutch Airlines)

KOREAN AIR (KE/KAL)   South Korea

Korean Air was formed in June 1962 to succeed Korean National Airlines (formed in 1948). The carrier was originally wholly owned by the Government of Korea, but was acquired by the Han Jin Group in 1969. Having found a need for an aircraft type to supplement its fleet of Boeing 747's, the airline placed an order for three Douglas DC-10-30s in 1974. Deliveries took place between February and April of the following year. Another two were obtained several years later, one being the sole example of the then recently defunct Air Siam, whilst the other was from Overseas National. It was the latter example which was lost in an accident at Anchorage in December 1983, thus reducing the DC-10 fleet from five to four. This remained static until 1988, when an example was leased from Japan Air System. In 1989 the type was reduced once again to four, when one crashed in fog at Tripoli. For most of the time, the aircraft link Seoul with the Middle East, Japan, the Philippines, Singapore, Hawaii and Libya. A European schedule is also maintained to Zurich. Today, Korean Air operates an extensive international network of scheduled passenger and cargo services linking Seoul with Frankfurt, London (LGW), Paris (ORY), and Zurich in Europe; Los Angeles, New York (JFK), Toronto, and Vancouver in North America; Bahrain, Jeddah, and Riyadh in the Middle East; and Bangkok, Fukuoka, Hong Kong, Kuala Lumpur, Manila, Nagasaki, Magoya, Nigata, Osaka, Singapore, Taipei and Tokyo (NRT) in Asia. In addition, domestic services link Seoul with Cheju and Pusan. The stunning Korean Air image was unveiled in early 1984. It was designed to replace the previous, somewhat dull, red, blue and white 'Korean Air Lines' scheme, which dated back to the 'sixties. In an unusual step for a major carrier, it was decided not only to change the livery design, but to adopt a completely new company motif and more dynamic title, all in one move. A pale shade of blue colours the entire upper fuselage half, representing the sky, below which runs a silver cheatline, with the underside in pale grey. Korean Air's logo, known as the 'Taeguk', combining the red and blue of heaven and earth (with white added to represent the 'endless strength of progress'), appears on the tail fin and forms the letter 'O' within the blue 'Korean Air' fuselage titles. The carrier's ICAO call sign is 'KOREANAIR'. *(K. G. Wright)*

LAKER AIRWAYS (GK)   United Kingdom

Laker Airways was formed in March 1966 by Sir Freddie Laker, to operate contract inclusive tour and *ad hoc* charter services. Operations began later that year. In 1971 Laker planned a cheap, no-frills, service from London to New York, called 'Skytrain'. It was originally decided to operate the route using Boeing 707 equipment, but such was the delay in receiving the required permission that two Douglas DC-10-10s were acquired, these coming from a cancelled Japanese order. So it was that on November 21, 1972, Laker operated its, and Europe's, first revenue earning service flown by a wide-bodied trijet. With a total of 331 passengers, G-AZZC, 'Southern Belle', flew to Majorca. The first two DC-10s delivered to the company were furnished with 345 yellow seats in a nine-breast arrangement, and a total of 10 cabin staff looked after the occupants. At that time the colour yellow was deemed fashionable, although by today's standards, it would look very out of place. By mid-1974, Skytrain had still not commenced, despite UK approval, and with the arrival of Laker's third DC-10, capacity was increased by 20 per cent. Some of this however, was used for IT work for the travel trade, including Laker's own associated companies, although it was deemed necessary to find further sources of employment so that the aircraft could be kept active. International Caribbean Airways helped to contribute in a small way, while a lease was negotiated with the Luxembourg-based Air Europe International for the DC-10s to fly between Europe and Tijuana in Mexico. As it so happened, the company called off its plans, leaving Laker to seek work elsewhere. Finally, after many years of waiting, Skytrain received its U.S. approval in June 1977, the first departure scheduled to leave Stansted on September 26. Following a number of appeals, the inaugural sevice departed Gatwick (the airport being changed from the original applied for) at 5.35pm GMT on Monday, September 26, 1977. Further expansion plans became possible in the following year when the CAA awarded Laker the Los Angeles route to operate as. a Skytrain service. Utilizing the Series 10 aircraft, a refuelling stop was necessary at Bangor, Maine, although this was eliminated when Laker took delivery of five DC-10-30s towards the end of 1979. Sadly, in February 1982 the company ceased trading. A total of ten DC-10s were grounded at Gatwick, whilst the remaining aircraft was stranded at Manchester. At that time the Laker fleet consisted of BAe 1-11, Douglas DC-10 and Airbus A300B4 aircraft. Most of the Series 10s found new homes almost straight away. However, all five of the Series 30s returned to the USA to spend two or three years in store at Long Beach or Yuma, before being sold to other carriers. Seen here, at London's Gatwick Airport, is one of the Laker 'Skytrain' DC-10s. *(B. J. Eagles)*

LAN CHILE (LA/LAN)   Chile

LAN Chile was formed by the Chilean Government on March 6, 1929, as Linea Aeropostal Santiago-Arica, and took its present name in 1932, when it became an autonomous state entity. In 1974 the company was the first to link South America with Australia via the South Pole, in an eleven hour, sixteen minute experimental flight. Having ordered two DC-10-30s for its international routes in 1981, LAN Chile leased-in N81NA from Pan Am, until its own were delivered in June 1982. Configured with a three-class layout, to accommodate a total of 262 passengers, the aircraft was used on the Chilean flag carrier's mid-week service between Frankfurt, Paris (ORY), Madrid, Rio de Janeiro, Buenos Aires and Santiago. At weekends it took over LAN Chile's Santiago-Miami-New York (JFK) schedules. LAN Chile completed another first in September 1986, when it carried out the first ever twinjet (a Boeing 767-200ER, CC-CJU) revenue service across the South Atlantic, from Rio de Janeiro to Madrid. The airline operates international scheduled passenger and cargo services from Santiago to Buenos Aires, Montevideo, Sao Paulo, Caracas, Rio de Janeiro, Lima, La Paz, Miami, New York

(JFK), Montreal, Los Angeles, Panama, Madrid, Papeete, and Santa Cruz. Domestic services are also operated from Santiago to Arica, Easter Island, Iquique, Calama, Antofagasta, El Salvador, Concepcion, Puerto Montt, Temuco, Copiago, and Punta Arenas. An all-Boeing fleet of 707-300, 737-200 and 767-200ER aircraft is operated. LAN Chile's colour scheme consists of bright patriotic shades of red, white and blue, which colours the very smart triple cheatline. This commences under the nose and continues along the fuselage, ultimately encompassing the entire fin. LAN Chile titling is displayed in white on the tail, reversed out of the blue, and in red on the forward cabin roof, alongside a white star in a red and blue disk. It should be noted that the Chilean flag appears under the cockpit windows. The carrier's sole pure-freighter Boeing 707, CC-CEB, sports additional 'Cargo' titles on the forward fuselage. Seen here is CC-CJT, a DC-10-30, at Miami International Airport. The aircraft was subsequently sold to American Airlines as N164AA, when LAN Chile replaced the type with Boeing 767-200ERs. The carrier's ICAO call sign is 'LAN CHILE'. *(K. G. Wright)*

LUFTHANSA (LH/DLH)

West Germany

Deutsche Luft Hansa Aktiengesellschaft was founded on January 6, 1926, as a result of a merger between Deutsche Aero Lloyd and Junkers Luftverkehr AG. The carrier's winged crest however, originated as far back as 1919, with Deutsche Luftrederei. In 1928, Luft Hansa established the first cargo service using aircraft strictly for this purpose. At the same time it employed the company's first steward on the Berlin-Paris route. Following an annual general meeting, a decision was made on June 30, 1933, to change the spelling of the company to Deutsche Lufthansa Aktiengesellschaft. With the outbreak of World War II in 1939, Lufthansa was forced to cease all international flights, and the following year it was required to sell all charter aircraft to the Aviation Ministry. Five years later, the company stopped all flights, and the airline was liquidated. In 1953, Luftag was founded for the purpose of establishing a new air transport system, and on August 6, 1954, a name change was made to Lufthansa German Airlines. Over the next year, Lufthansa began providing scheduled domestic flights in the Federal Republic of Germany. Services to foreign destinations were inaugurated soon afterwards. In the years that followed, Lufthansa claimed many firsts.

These included being the first airline to put the Boeing 737 City Jet into service, and the first European carrier to operate Boeing 747s. 1978 saw the company strengthen its involvement in regional air transport by investing in DLT, and by 1987 Lufthansa had acquired interests in Viva, Hapag Lloyd, Amadeus and Cargolux. That same year, the carrier undertook an internal reorganization to cut overheads and streamline operations and sales. The Federal German Government currently holds 74 per cent of Lufthansa's shares, whilst the remainder is held by the State of North Rhine-Westphalia, Federal German Railways and private investors. Today, the West German flag carrier maintains a fleet of Douglas DC-10, Boeing 727, 737, 747, Airbus A300, A310, and A320 aircraft. An order is outstanding for up to thirty of the Airbus A340 type, as well as a number of the Airbus A321. Lufthansa operates an extensive worldwide system of scheduled passenger and cargo services to 149 points in 78 countries, in Europe, Africa, the Near, Middle and Far East, Australia, and North, Central and South America. Seen here is a Douglas DC-10-30 on push-back from Frankfurt Airport. The carrier's ICAO call sign is 'LUFTHANSA'. *(B. T. Richards)*

MALAYSIA AIRLINES (MH/MAS)   Malaysia

In August 1976, Malaysia Airlines claimed a point-to-point record, when its first Douglas DC-10-30 was delivered. The route that the aircraft took was from Honolulu to Kuala Lumpur, non stop. Once established within the carrier's fleet, the type was put onto long haul services, which included those in Europe. A third example was ordered in 1979 for delivery in February 1981, but in the following year, the arrival of a pair of Boeing 747-236s from British Airways, relegated the DC-10s to the regional routes around the Far East. This however has changed, and the type can be seen regularly at the European destinations served, as well as on charter services to the UK. Seen here is a DC-10-30 at Frankfurt Airport. The aircraft had recently arrived from Kuala Lumpur, and is depicted on its first visit to the German destination after having been painted in its new company livery. The previous colour scheme consisted of dual red cheatlines above and below the windowline. This was derived from the Malaysian flag which carried 14 red and white horizontal stripes, with a crescent moon and star on a blue field in the top left corner. The symbol then, and now, of Malaysia Airlines, which appears on the fin of the airline's aircraft is a stylized Kelantan Kite. Traditionally this has been a spectacular expression of Malaysian mastery of controlled flight. As such it is the essence of everything that the airline represents: the feeling for controlled flight, for movement, for tradition and for Malaysian cultural heritage. Malaysians have flown the Kelantan Kite for thousands of years, and it was thus deemed to be the perfect symbol for the national carrier. Now, in its modern streamlined form, the kite symbolizes a new way to fly to the country. The carrier's ICAO call sign is 'MALAYSIAN'. *(K. G. Wright)*

MALAYSIAN AIRLINE SYSTEM (MH/MAS)

Malaysia

Malaysian Airline System was formed in April 1971 after the ending of the Malaysia-Singapore Airlines consortium, and operations began on October 1, 1972. The national carrier began operations as a wholly owned Government entity but, following a privatization exercise at the end of 1985, the Malaysian Government's equity participation was reduced to 70 per cent. This was then further reduced and by March 31, 1987, the Government's shareholding stood at 52 per cent — comprising 42 per cent held by Minister of Finance (Incorporated) and 5 per cent each for the Sarawak and Sabah State Governments. MAS operates an extensive network of scheduled domestic flights to 34 points, plus international services to Singapore, Jakarta, Hatyai, Bandar Seri Begawan, Medan, Manila, Hong Kong, Taipei, Tokyo (NRT), Dubai, Amman, Colombo, Denpassar, Bangkok, Melbourne, Perth, Sydney, Madras, Seoul, Honolulu, Los Angeles, Amsterdam, Jeddah, London (LHR), Frankfurt, and Paris (CDG). The airline has equity participation in three major associate companies, Pan Pacific Hotel in Kuala Lumpur, Malaysia Helicopter Services, and Pelangi Air Sdn Bhd, Malaysia's new domestic airline, which started operations in January 1988. MAS operates a fleet of Boeing 737, 747, Airbus A300, Fokker F-27, F-50 and DHC-6 Twin Otter aircraft. On order are several examples of the Boeing 747-400, which will help give the airline increased capacity. The red and white stripes of the national flag are reproduced as twin bold cheatlines, and are separated by a narrow white windowline. The fuselage bottom is painted grey on the Boeing 747s and A300s, natural metal and grey on the DC-10s, natural metal on the Boeing 737s and white on the smaller domestic types. An all red fin portrays a white central disk, which contains the traditional Kalantan Kite motif, and overlooks the all white fuselage top and red lower case 'Malaysian' titles. Two flags appear, preceding the titles on the port side and following them on the starboard; one has Islamic significance and the other is the national flag. Seen here on arrival at Hong Kong's Kai Tak International Airport· on October 7, 1987, is Douglas DC-10-30, PK-GIB. The aircraft was on lease from the Indonesian airline, Garuda. This example's sistership, PK-GIA, can be found under the Garuda Indonesia heading. The carrier's ICAO call sign is 'MALAYSIAN'.
(B. J. Eagles)

MARTINAIR HOLLAND (MP/MPH)

Netherlands

Martinair was formed in May 1958 as Martin's Air Charter, and the present title was adopted in 1974. The airline was an early operator of the DC-10-30CF combi, having ordered one aircraft in early 1972, for delivery the following year. For its passenger role, 345 seats were specified, with their removal for freight work taking approximately 12 hours. A specially designed pallet loading system was installed incorporating on-board electric winches, which to some extent made it independent of ground facilities. A large proportion of Martinair's business is derived from subcontracts. Most of the fleet have seen service with many varied airlines, that include Garuda Indonesia, Virgin Atlantic, and Qantas. By the end of 1976, three DC-10s were in service, operating in an all-freight role due to recession of the IT market. Following a recovery in the industry, a larger number of passenger charters were flown world-wide, destinations including the ever popular Mediterranean area and the Canaries. The company operates scheduled transatlantic passenger services from Amsterdam to Baltimore, Detroit, Los Angeles, Miami, Minneapolis, New York (JFK), San Francisco, Seattle and Toronto. The major part of the company's business, however, is the operation of worldwide passenger and cargo charters. In addition, the company provides complete inclusive-tour packages and operates air-taxi and executive flights. Martinair maintains and operates the Dutch Government's Fokker F-28, used by members of the Royal Family and the Cabinet. Shareholders are Royal Nedlloyd Group (49.2 per cent), KLM (28.8 per cent) and various financial institutions (21 per cent). Associate companies are active in the fields of flight training, sales support by hostess teams (they helped, for example, British Midland when they first introduced their London (LHR)-Amsterdam route), party catering and the production of deep freeze meals and components. In Amsterdam the MartINN restaurant is operated. A fleet of Douglas DC-10-30CF, Airbus A310-200, Boeing 747-200, Boeing 767-300ER, McDonnell Douglas MD82, Cessna 550 Citation II and Cessna 404 Titan aircraft is operated. The latter type, PH-MPC, is operated for the Dutch Coast Guard. Martinair's first Boeing 767-300ER, PH-MCG, was delivered in September 1989, whilst PH-MCH arrived in March 1990. McDonnell Douglas DC-10-30CF, PH-MBT, and MD-82, PH-MBZ, were sold to Global Leasing SpA of Curaçao on January 5, 1989, and were immediately leased back. The DC-10 was wet leased to KLM for a period of thirty months, between October 17, 1989, and April 30, 1992. Depicted here, at Amsterdam's Schipol Airport, is Douglas DC-10-30, PH-MBN. 'Anthony Ruys' was taxiing just prior to its departure for Baltimore. The aircraft was sold to Guinness Peat Aviation, but has been leased back for the next few years. The carrier's ICAO call sign is 'MARTINAIR'. *(K. G. Wright)*

MEXICANA (MX/MXA)   Mexico

Mexicana claims to be the the second oldest airline in America, and the fourth oldest in the world. Founded as Compania Mexicana de Transportes Aereos in 1921, the carrier adopted its present name on August 20, 1924, with a base at Tampico, utilizing four Lincoln Standard aircraft, Scheduled operations began on April 15, 1928, connecting Mexico City, Tampico and Tuxpan. In March 1929 Charles Lindbergh piloted the carrier's first international flight between Mexico City and Brownville, via Tampico. During its early years Mexicana was owned primarily by Pan American, with the last Pan Am holdings relinquished in 1967. Company acquisitions include Aerovias Centrales in December 1935, and Transportes Aereos de Jaliaco in 1955. The airline entered the jet age with Comet equipment in July 1960, began Boeing 727 services in 1967, and introduced the DC-10 into its network in 1981. The latter was of the Series 15 variety. Mexicana, along with Aeromexico, were the only two carriers to operate this type. This enabled both Mexican airlines to maintain widebodied flights to some of the South American high altitude airports, which it would not normally have been possible to serve with such a large passenger load. Mexicana has a total of five 315-seat types on strength. The first three of these were delivered in 1981, with the other two following in 1983. Today,

it operates scheduled passenger and cargo services to 31 points in Mexico, and to Los Angeles, Denver, Dallas/Ft. Worth, San Antonio, Tampa, Chicago, Miami, San Francisco, Seattle, Baltimore/Washington, and Philadelphia in the USA; plus Havana, San Juan, Guatemala City, and San Jose (Costa Rica). The Mexican Government became the major shareholder in the carrier when it increased its holdings to 58 per cent on July 15, 1982. However, is likely to sell these to the private sector in the near future. A fleet of Douglas DC-10-15, and Boeing 727-200 aircraft are operated. The company's striking livery was inspired by Mexico's famous Aztec history. A broad 'Aztec' cheatline sweeps along the entire fuselage length, trimmed either side in black, underlining bold black 'Mexicana' titling and the national flag, complete with flagpole. The theme continues on the fin which is dominated by a black stylized Eagle logo in the form of an 'M' initial. It should be noted that additional 'Mexicana' titles are sported on the third engine of the DC-10, but not on the Boeing 727s, and that engines number one and two of both types are painted gold. Seen here is one of the five DC-10-15s maintained by Mexicana. The aircraft is depicted at Miami, having made a flight from Mexico City, The carrier's ICAO call sign is 'MEXICANA'.
(K. G. Wright)

NATIONAL AIRLINES (NA)

United States of America

National Airlines, the Miami-based carrier, was formèd in 1934. It covered a large network of domestic routes, which embraced a total of fifteen states in America. The carrier was an early customer for the Douglas DC-10-10. Eleven of this type were ordered for use on its trunk sectors, with N60NA becoming the first to be delivered in November 1971. National had inaugurated its newly-acquired London route in June 1970, and in due course the carrier positioned the type on its transatlantic services to Heathrow, Paris, Zurich, Frankfurt and Amsterdam. For this purpose the airline found it necessary to acquire four of the longer range Series 30 aircraft. Two were delivered in June 1973, with the others following two years later. During the late 1970s the airline became a favourable target for several expanding carriers, and eventually became a subsidiary of Pan Am on January 7, 1980, prior to being completely taken over by its new owner. National Airlines adopted its unique livery in December 1967, when Gene Moore of Tiffany Inc. was commissioned to design a new corporate emblem and livery to reflect the sunshine oasis of Florida. This resulted in a stunning orange, lemon and lime livery. The first aircraft to adopt this scheme was a Douglas DC-8-21, N6572C, 'Sally', which flew on the New York-Florida route. In 1972, National introduced a marketing campaign under the slogan 'Fly Me', relating this to its airliners by personally identifying the whole fleet with girls names, chosen from the names of the airline stewardesses. These individual names appeared on the aircraft in large coloursplash name scrolls above the flightdeck windows. The marketing campaign featured wording such as 'I'm Sue — Fly Me', the words applying equally to the flight attendant or the plane in the advertisement. Boeing 747-135, N77772, 'Patricia', made National's first translantic flight from Miami to London, on May 26, 1972. Prior to the airline being taken over by Pan Am, a fleet of Douglas DC-10 and Boeing 727 aircraft were utilized. *(Author's Collection)*

NIGERIA AIRWAYS (WT/NGA)   Nigeria

Nigeria Airways, the national flag carrier of the oil rich African country of Nigeria, was founded in 1958, to take over all Nigerian services formerly operated by West African Airways Corporation. Today the carrier is wholly-owned by the Nigerian Federal Government and serves destinations in East and West Africa. International flights are operated from Lagos, Kano and Port Harcourt to London (LHR), Amsterdam, Paris (ORY), Rome, New York (JFK) and Jeddah. A large domestic network links all of the nineteen states in the Nigerian Federation, with key cities in the country. The route map includes Benin, Calabour, Enugu, Jos, Maiduguri, Port Harcourt, Sokoto, Abuja, Yola, Makurdi, Kano, Ilorin and Kaduna. Nigeria Airways operates a fleet of Douglas DC-10, Boeing 707, 737, Airbus A310, Fokker F-27 and ATR-42 types. One of the carrier's Douglas DC-10-30s is pictured here having just departed from London's Heathrow Airport in November 1986. The green and white livery of Nigeria Airways was provided by the national flag, which itself appears on the tail. With it is the superimposed 'flying elephant' company logo. Two green cheatlines are separated by a narrow white windowline and underline the bold green 'Nigerian Airways' fuselage lettering, which all appear in upper case. The lower fuselage is left in a natural metal, contrasting starkly with the white roof, on all types except the A310, which has a grey underside. Delivery of the airline's first Douglas DC-10 took place in October 1976. From the beginning, 300 seats were installed in all economy layout, since its first duty was to be a part of the annual Mecca pilgrims' shuttle. Once completed, the aircraft was returned to a more normal 272-seat layout. In January 1987, the airline was unlucky enough to lose 5N-ANR, during a training session, so a replacement was therefore necessary. In the interim period a Boeing 747 was leased from SAS, whilst the A310s supplemented the DC-10 on long haul routes. During 1989, Nigeria Airways became the recipient of the last DC-10-30. Registered N3024W, the aircraft was originally to have been given the registration 5N-ALR, although this was not taken up. The carrier's ICAO call sign is 'NIGERIAN'. *(K. G. Wright)*

NORTHWEST AIRLINES (NW/NWA)
United States of America

The airline was formed in August 1926 as Northwest Airways, and adopted the title Northwest Orient Airlines in 1934. The company was reorganized in 1985 to form NWA Inc. as a holding company for Northwest Airlines and several other subsidiaries. In October 1985 it became the launch customer for the Boeing 747-400, and a year later ordered up to 100 Airbus Industrie A320 aircraft. The carrier merged with Republic Airlines on August 2, 1986, thus strengthening the airline's US route system, with major domestic traffic hubs at Detroit (Michigan), Minneapolis/St. Paul (Minnesota), Memphis (Tennessee). The company has marketing agreements with various airlines who operate feeder services under the name 'Northwest Airlink'. Northwest operates an extensive network of scheduled passenger and cargo services in the USA and Canada. Transpacific services are operated to Hawaii, Tokyo (NRT), Osaka, Seoul, Okinawa, Taipei, Manila, Hong Kong, Shangai, Guam, Singapore (cargo only), and Bangkok. Transatlantic flights serve London (LGW), Frankfurt, and several other points in Europe. The carrier also maintains operations to Cancun and Puerto Vallarta (Mexico), Montego Bay (Jamaica), and the Cayman Islands. A fleet of Douglas DC-10, DC-9, McDonnell Douglas MD82, Boeing 727, 747, 757, and Airbus Industrie A320 aircraft is maintained. Orders for the Airbus A330 and A340 to replace certain types within the fleet are outstanding. In 1989 Northwest became the first airline to put the Boeing 747-400 into commercial service, be it only on domestic flights for crew training. The aircraft were subsequently put on to transpacific operations to Tokyo (NRT). A new Northwest Airlines livery was adopted during that year. In a move away from its normal bare metal aircraft, the carrier now uses a four-tone colour scheme. The first band, coloured red, covers the tail and top of the fuselage, whilst the second, coloured grey, acts as a cheatline, and runs to the aircraft nose. The third band is a black stripe that runs the entire length of the fuselage, breaking up the grey tone from the fourth colour, white, which adorns the underside of the fuselage. Large 'Northwest' titles, in capitals, are situated on the forward fuselage, whilst on the tail the company logo, a letter 'N' in a white circle with a pointer showing 'northwest', appears. The carrier's ICAO call sign is 'NORTHWEST'. *(B. T. Richards)*

NOVAIR INTERNATIONAL AIRWAYS (EN/NGK)

United Kingdom

Novair International Airways was originally registered as British Caledonian Airways (Prestwick) Ltd in 1961. In 1982 the name Cal Air International was adopted. Today, the carrier, a charter Operator, based at London's Gatwick Airport, is owned by the Rank Organisation. British Airways had a fifty per cent shareholding, when the company took over the assets from the merger of British Caledonian Airways; however in 1988 these were subsequently sold. At the end of the same year it was decided that due to the name of British Airways' charter subsidiary, Caledonian Airways, the airline would change its name to Novair International Airways. This would stop any confusion and allow the carrier to 'spread its wings'. The company operates regular passenger charters to Europe and North American destinations, from Gatwick, Manchester, Newcastle, Glasgow and Birmingham. *Ad hoc* charters are also operated. A fleet of three wide-bodied Douglas DC-10-10s are operated, two former Laker aircraft, and one purchased from American Trans Air. In 1989 two Boeing 737-46B's were added, thus enabling Novair to economize on routes where the DC-10 was too large. Seen here is G-GCAL, the DC-10 bought from American Trans Air. The aircraft was only the second airframe built of this type. With construction number 46501, it should have been delivered to American Airlines as N101AA in 1972, but this order was not taken up. McDonnell Douglas re-registered the aircraft as N10DC, and it was used for autoland systems trials. In June 1977, it was sold to Laker Airways as G-BELO, for use on the company's new 'Skytrain' service to New York (JFK), and was named 'Southern Belle'. When the carrier ceased operations in 1982, it was sold to American Trans Air as N183AT in February 1983. The livery as depicted here is modern, colourful and distinctive, although it is not the current one. This features a bold bright red sash, which has been trimmed below by a deep blue pinstripe, over a fresh white fuselage. It is completed by a diagonal 'Novair' titling in deep blue and white. A falling star dominates the tail. The carrier's ICAO call sign is 'NOVAIR'. It should be noted that Novair ceased all operations on May 5, 1990, due to a downturn in passenger levels.

(K. G. Wright)

OVERSEAS NATIONAL AIRWAYS (ON/ONA)

United States of America

In June 1950 Overseas National Airways was founded by George Tomkins, utilizing Douglas DC-6s and DC-7s, on Air Force Contracts. By 1960 it had become the biggest and most respected non-scheduled airline in the business, claiming to fly more international passenger miles than any other US carrier, with the exception of Pan Am. Through uneconomical price setting, ONA went bankrupt on October 29, 1963, and ceased operations. The carrier was not disgraced, and did not loose its certificate. With the efforts of Steedman Hinckley, it was revived following refinancing from various banking interests, and operations were resumed on October 4, 1965, with new Douglas DC-8s being purchased in 1966. In March 1966 a permanent domestic authority was granted for the carrier. This included Inclusive Tour Charter, as well as other group and full plane charters. The same order also granted worldwide military charters. In April 1966, permission was granted for transatlantic charters, thus enabling ONA to access the very market it was hoping for, followed in September of the same year by the granting of licenses to the Caribbean. Sharing the honour of receiving the first convertible Douglas DC-10 with Trans International on April 17, 1973, Overseas National had two in service by the end of that June. The main usage of the aircraft was long haul freight and passenger charters, the latter frequently being involved in flying tourists to Europe. During the autumn of 1975, ONA lost one of its fleet, DC-1030CF, N1032F 'Holidayliner Freedom', when a flock of birds stupidly decided to make an inspection of the interior of one of the engines during take-off at New York's JFK International. This was followed soon afterwards by the remaining example, DC-10-30CF, N1031F 'Holidayliner America', suffering a landing accident at Istanbul on January 12, 1976. Two replacements were acquired in 1977, Series 30, N1033F 'Holidayliner Enterprise', and Series 30, N1034F 'Holidayliner Liberty'. This was followed by a third example in 1978, Series 30CF, N1035F, which arrived just before the carrier suspended operations. Passing through various hands, N1033F ended its days in the hands of Korean Air as HL7339. It was written off at Anchorage on December 23, 1983. N1034F was with Spantax as EC-DEG, when it was written off at Malaga on September 13, 1982. The only 'survivor' is N1035F which is now being operated as an all-freight aircraft by Federal Express, as N304FE. The company was dissolved on September 7, 1978, with its certificate being withdrawn on May 19, 1982. Seen here in August 1978 is N1034F, just prior to landing at Paris (ORY) Airport. (Aviation Photo News)

PAKISTAN INTERNATIONAL AIRLINES (PK/PIA)

Pakistan

Pakistan International Airlines was founded in 1954 and became a corporation in March 1955 when the company was merged with Orient Airways (founded in 1946). The carrier operates scheduled passenger and cargo services to 40 destinations in 37 countries, as well as 32 domestic points. International stations include: Abu Dhabi, Bahrain, Dhaka, Beijing, Copenhagen, Dubai, Cairo, Frankfurt, Paris (ORY), Athens, Delhi, Bombay, Tehran, Baghdad, Rome, Tokyo (NRT), Amman, Nairobi, Kuwait, Tripoli, Kuala Lumpur, Kathmandu, Amsterdam, Muscat, Manila, Doha, Jeddah, Dhahran, Riyadh, Singapore, Columbo, Damascus, Bangkok, Istanbul, Moscow (SVO), London (LHR), New York (JFK), Manchester, Male, Toronto, and Sana'a. The Government is the principal shareholder with 62 per cent, the remainder of the shares being held primarily by institutions. PIA's introduction to the wide-bodied era came in 1974, when Douglas delivered three DC-10-30s to the fleet. Originally equipped with 229 seats, this arrangement was changed in 1975 by removing some of the cargo space on the upper deck to give an increased capacity of 277. A fourth aircraft was delivered in 1976, and this number remained constant until February 1981, when AP-AXE was lost in an accident at Karachi. Two years later the total was restored, with the arrival of an aircraft from the Italian carrier, Alitalia. The aircraft, however, had a relatively brief stay with PIA. In 1985, following negotiations with CP Air, the company disposed of its entire DC-10 fleet to the Canadian carrier, in exchange for four

Boeing 747s, This process was phased throughout 1986. The current fleet consists of Boeing 707, 737, 747, Fokker F-27, DHC-6 Twin Otter, and Airbus A300 types. An order for Airbus Industrie A310-300's is outstanding, pending delivery during the 'nineties, which will enable the Pakistani carrier to phase-out its fleet of Boeing 707s. PIA's livery is based upon the colours of the national flag. The basic livery has always comprised green since the company was formed in 1955. The original cheatline on the aircraft featured a Sabre styling and this was carried on the Hawker Siddeley 121 Trident jets when they were introduced, and on the original jet services operated by Boeing 707-320s. These aircraft were leased from Pan American, but in full PIA livery, which operated the first jet service to London (LHR) from Karachi, via Tehran, Beirut, Rome and Geneva, on October 4, 1960. At this time the fin livery comprised the PIA white motif with a line of white stars above and below the PIA on an all green fin. A livery modification took place in 1975, when this double line of stars was removed from the colour scheme as the first step in a complete modernization programme and livery redesign. The current livery of green and gold, was designed by consultants, Negus and Negus. It was introduced on PIA's first Boeing 747 on May 1, 1976. Seen here is DC-10-30, AP-BBL. The aircraft is now with Canadian International, as C-FCRE 'Empress of Canada'. The carrier's ICAO call sign is 'PAKISTAN'. *(K. G. Wright)*

PAN AMERICAN   United States of America
WORLD AIRWAYS (PA/PAA)

Pam Am was originally formed in March 1927 to operate a United States Parcel Service contract between Key West, in Florida, and Havana, in Cuba. Following a period of rapid route expansion, the carrier's network soon took in points throughout the Caribbean, Central and South America. In due course, Trans-Pacific and Trans-Atlantic services were inaugurated using flying boats. With the takeover of National Airlines in January 1980, Pan Am gained an assorted fleet of DC-10s. These comprised a mixture of series 10s and Series 30s. It was a desire to increase its involvement in US domestic services that was the principle reason for the purchase. Therefore it was not long before Pam Am's livery was displayed on the aircraft. These could be found plying routes along the eastern seaboard of America. National had previously used its DC-10s on international sectors such as Miami-London (LHR), and these, too, continued uninterrupted for a while. However, a change of policy brought about a fleet standardization. This entailed all tri-jets leaving the fleet from the end of 1983. All DC-10s were transfrerred to American Airlines, with the exception of N84NA, which found a home with United Airlines. Today Pan Am is one of the world's major carriers, with a route network that covers around fifty-six

points in the USA, fourteen in South America, plus Europe, the Middle East, India and Pakistan. It is one of the largest operators at New York (JFK). Following the loss of the Pacific division, Pan Am has concentrated on expanding its transatlantic services. A further nine European destinations .(Leningrad, Moscow (SVO), Milan, Helsinki, Oslo, Stockholm, Prague, Krakov, and Shannon) were added in 1986, bringing the number of European points to forty. A network of local services to Germany is also operated. In December 1986, the carrier became the first US airline to link the USA and Saudi Arabia directly, with a same aircraft New York (JFK)-Frankfurt-Riyadh service. Pan Am operates a fleet of Boeing 727, 737, 747, ATR-42, Airbus A300 and A310 types. In 1989 the company cancelled an order for up to fifty Airbus A320s, due to financial difficulties. The units from the production line were transferred to Braniff; however, the latter carrier filed for Chapter 11 bankruptcy in 1989, and the aircraft were sold to other airlines. Seen here is a Douglas DC-10-30, in full Pan Am colour scheme. The aircraft was operating a flight from Miami to London (LHR), as PA 98. Pan Am's ICAO call sign is 'CLIPPER'. *(K. G. Wright)*

PHILIPPINE AIRLINES (PR/PAL)

Philippines

Philippine Airlines began limited operations on March 15, 1941, only to be interrupted a few months later by the Second World War. Domestic services recommenced on February 14, 1946, using war surplus Douglas DC-3 equipment, with international flights being introduced a year later. Long-range routes were suspended in 1954, and until 1961 PAL operated only within the Philippine Islands and to Hong Kong. Today, the carrier operates scheduled passenger and cargo services over a 41 point domestic system, together with international flights to Singapore, Kuala Lumpur, Taipei, Hong Kong, Honolulu, San Francisco, Los Angeles, Chicago, Tokyo (NRT), Melbourne, Sydney, Brisbane, Ho Chi Minh City, Bangkok, Karachi, Frankfurt, Amsterdam, Paris (ORY), Zurich, Beijing, Xiamen, Dhahran, Dubai, and London (LGW). State shareholding in PAL was 24.6 per cent until November 1977, when the Government State Insurance System acquired the 74 per cent interest held by Rubicom (owned by the Toda family). Government holding is now 99.7 per cent. A fleet of Douglas DC-10, Boeing 747, Airbus A300, BAe 1-11, BAe 748, Shorts 360 and Fokker 50 aircraft is maintained. PAL's latest livery, as worn by the Boeing 747s, takes its colours from the crimson and blue national flag and features twin broad cheatlines separated by a narrow white windowline. The tail-fin is entirely encompassed by a stylized upturned representation of the Philippine flag, although the traditional yellow stars have been omitted for the sake of style. The white upper fuselage displays black 'Philippine Airlines' titles alongside the national flag, and the lower fuselage finish is natural metal, often highly polished. The carrier's A300s wear a similar livery but with a white fuselage underside. The Douglas DC-10s, however, still sport the company's previous livery variation, incorporating much narrower cheatlines. Seen here on its impressive landing at Hong Kong's Kai Tak Airport is Douglas DC-10-30, RP-C2114. The airline's ICAO call sign is 'PHILIPPINE'. *(B. J. Eagles)*

SABENA — BELGIAN WORLD AIRLINES (SN/SAB)

Belgium

Sabena was founded in 1923 as a successor to SNETA, and developed a European network followed by routes to and within the Belgian Congo (now Zaire). The airline's first Douglas DC-10-30 Combi was delivered in September 1973, and entered service on the North Atlantic run on November 1 of that year. With the return of two Boeing 747-100s from a conversion programme, these flights ceased in the Spring of 1974. The DC-10 took over the routes that linked Brussels with the Far East, until the introduction of a sister-ship, which enabled the expansion of the type's activities to include some African sectors from July 1. By 1980, a total of five DC-10s were in service. They have since been returned to some of the American and Canadian services, whilst the Boeing 747s have been given the responsibility of the busier African sectors. In 1987 negotiations took place with Scandinavian Airlines (SAS) on the possibility of combining the two carrier's transatlantic operations, as well as catering, hotel, and other interests. A merger, however, did not result. A number of joint venture discussions have been held with various airlines since then. The Belgian Government owns 54 per cent of the equity in the carrier, with banks and insurance companies being the other shareholders. Sabena operates an extensive network of scheduled passenger and cargo services to points in Europe, the Middle and Far East, 26 destinations in Africa and to Montreal, New York (JFK), Atlanta, Detroit, Chicago, Boston, Toronto and Anchorage. The airline has extended its African network by adding new services to Niamey (Niger), Lome (Togo), Cotonou (Benin), and Luanda (Angola). Subsidiaries include Sobelair, Société Transair Internationale, Sodehotel, Compagnie des Grands Hotels Africains, Compagnie Internationale de Gestion-Bruxelles, Sabena Catering Services, Belgian Fuelling and Services, Sabena Interservice Centre and Delta Air Transport. Sabena's livery was introduced on the occasion of the company's 50th anniversary in 1973 the tail design having been created by the airline's publicity department in Brussels. The 'birthday' was considered to be a suitable moment to revitalize the emblem which had been in existence for the previous 50 years. The Sabena blue was retained and the Belgian flag appears between the Sabena and Belgian World Airlines titling. The fin of each airliner carries in blue on a white circle the elongated capital 'S', the initial letter of the company's name. S also stands for service, and although this was indeed a chance coincidence, it was nonetheless symbolic of the ideal which animated the work of the employees of the airline. With the debut of the A310 in March 1984, it was decided to make a few changes to the livery. A new, lighter blue cheatline extends along the fuselage length, trimmed either side by narrow pinstripes in the same colour. Matching Sabena titles are displayed on the upper fuselage in a new style, but are still followed by the flag and 'Belgian World Airlines' subtitles. The tail fin design remains unaffected. The lower fuselage is painted grey in all cases. The Sabena fleet consists of Douglas DC-10, Boeing 737, 747 and Airbus A310 aircraft. An order for several Airbus A340-300s will be delivered from 1993 to replace the DC-10. The carrier's call sign is 'SABENA'. *(K. G. Wright)*

SAS — SCANDINAVIAN AIRLINES SYSTEM (SK/SAS)

Denmark, Norway, Sweden

In 1946 it was agreed that all overseas services of the national airlines of Denmark, Norway and Sweden, would be merged, to be operated by a single new airline, to be known as Scandinavian Airlines System. SAS was formed on July 31, 1946, and by October 1, 1950, the three carriers were fully integrated. The company is owned in the proportion of 2:2:3 by Det Danske Luftfartselskap (Danish Airlines), Det Norske Luftfartselskap (Norwegian Airlines), and Aerostransport (Swedish Airlines). These three limited companies are in turn, through shareholdings, owned fifty per cent by private individuals or enterprises, and fifty per cent by their respective national governments. Wholly-owned subsidiaries are SAS Service Partner (catering and offshore Services), SAS International Hotels, SAS Information and Reservation system, and SAS Leisure. Scanair is an associate company, jointly owned by ABA, DDL, and DNL, which operates charter and inclusive tour services. Other airlines in which SAS has an interest are Danair (57 per cent), Linjeflyg (50 per cent), Greenlandair (25 per cent), Wideroe (22 per cent), and

Helikopter Service (5 per cent). A fleet of Douglas DC-9, DC-10, Fokker F50, McDonnell Douglas MD 81, 82, 83, 87, and Boeing 767 aircraft is operated. An order for the MD11 is outstanding, pending delivery for the early 'nineties. An extensive network of Scandinavian and European scheduled passenger services is operated, together with routes to Africa, the Middle and Far East, North and South America. The colourful SAS livery was given board approval in 1983 in preference to two similar designs, and is now worn fleetwide. A white overall fuselage has, as its highlight, a rhombus in the national colours of the three participating nations, Denmark, Norway and Sweden (as read from the front). Simple 'Scandinavian' titles are in dark blue outlined in gold. This colouring is also the same for the 'SAS' tail logo. The three national flags appear on the rear engines or rear fuselage (reading Denmark, Norway, Sweden from left to right). The carrier's ICAO call sign is 'SCANDINAVIAN'.

(Scandinavian Airline System)

SCANAIR (DK/VKG)   Denmark, Norway, Sweden

Scanair was formed on June 30, 1961, as a Danish charter company, but on October 1, 1965, it was reorganized as a Scandinavian charter consortium, owned by ABA (Swedish Airlines), DDL (Danish Airlines), and DNL (Norwegian Airlines), in the proportion 3:2:2. Today, the carrier is Scandinavian Airlines System's charter subsidiary, and undertakes charter and inclusive-tour flights. These are mainly to destinations in the holiday centres of the Mediterranean, the Canary Islands, West Germany, Austria, France, United Kingdom, Switzerland and Gambia. Scanair maintains a fleet of Douglas DC-10 and DC-8 equipment. In addition to these, it also leases aircraft from SAS and Linjeflyg. Throughout the years, Scanair has operated many aircraft types, including the Boeing 747 and Airbus A300. The company livery has always reflected Scanair's close links with SAS, and the present scheme is no exception. It was unveiled in 1983, shortly after the new image of the parent company. The pure white fuselage displays a colourful flash, which instead of representing the flags of the participating nations, is painted in sunshine stripes of orange, below dark blue 'Scanair' titles, in the SAS style. The all-white fin simply displays a huge orange sun. The Danish, Norwegian and Swedish flags appear side by side on the rear fuselage, always in that sequence. In mid-1988 the carrier came to an agreement whereby it would lease a total of six Douglas DC-10-10s from United Aircraft Leasing. All aircraft were in service by early 1989, having been re-registered in Scandinavia prior to their introduction. Seen here is SE-DFH, a Douglas DC-10-30. 'Rurik Viking' is seen here at one of its Scandinavian points of call, resplendent in its very colourful livery. The aircraft was originally delivered to Air New Zealand in June 1976, as ZK-NZS. From there it was leased to Pan Am in April 1979, before being sold to International Lease Finance on June 29, 1982. The same day it was resold to Lan Chile as CC-CJS 'Santiago', before going to SAS, and then to its present owner. The carrier's ICAO call sign is 'VIKING'. *(K. G. Wright)*

SINGAPORE AIRLINES (SQ/SIA)   Singapore

Singapore Airlines was formed on January 25, 1972, as the wholly Government-owned national airline of Singapore, to succeed the jointly operated Malaysia-Singapore Airlines. Operations began on October 1 of that year. In November 1985 some sixteen per cent of SIA's expanded stock was sold to local and international investors. This reduced the Government's holding to seventy-five per cent in June 1987. The carrier's first two Boeing 747-400 'Megatop' aircraft were delivered in December 1988, and began non-stop Singapore to London (LHR) services in early 1989. SIA's first 747 pure freighter entered service in August of that year, operating to Europe, the Far East, and the south west Pacific. Subsidiary companies include Tradewinds, Singapore Airport Terminal Services, Singapore Engine Overhaul Centre, Singapore Aviation and General Insurance, Singapore International Software Services, Aeroformation Asia, and Singapore Properties. Scheduled passenger and cargo services are operated from Singapore to Auckland, Adelaide, Christchurch, Darwin, Port Moresby, Brisbane, Sydney, Melbourne, Perth, Honolulu, Los Angeles, San Francisco, Tokyo (NRT), Osaka, Seoul, Taipei (CKS), Hong Kong, Manila, Bandar Seri Begawan, Jakarta, Fukuoka, Medan, Kuala Lumpur, Kuantan, Penang, Bangkok, Columbo, Cairo, Calcutta, Kathmandu, Denpasar, Delhi, Dhaka, Male, Manchester, Dhahran, Bahrain, Athens, Rome, Vienna, Istanbul, Zurich, Frankfurt, Paris (CDG), Amsterdam, Copenhagen, Brussels and London (LHR). A fleet of Boeing 747 and Airbus Industrie A310 aircraft is maintained. A white fuselage displays shortened cheatlines in midnight blue and yellow, below blue upper case 'Singapore Airlines' titles. A large, stylized, yellow bird looks down from the mainly blue fin, which is repeated in miniature on each engine. Although Singapore Airlines no longer operates the Douglas DC-10, 9V-SDD is depicted here at Changi International Airport, during March 1980. A Series 30, the aircraft was purchased new by the flag carrier on March 30, 1979, and stayed with the airline until 1983. On August 9 of that year, it was sold to Bangladesh Biman as S2-ACP, 'City of Dacca'. The carrier's ICAO call sign is 'SINGAPORE'.

(Aviation Photo News)

SPANTAX (BX/BXS)   Spain

Spantax was formed in October 1959, initially to support operations for oil-prospecting companies in the Spanish Sahara. General passenger charters were started three years later. These were considerably extended to inlude inclusive-tour services to Spain from various parts of Europe, as well as *ad hoc* charters world wide. The principal shareholder in the carrier was the Aviation Finance Group, along with the President of the carrier, Captain Rodolfo Bay, and Vice President Miss Marta Estades. Spantax had bases at Palma de Mallorca and Las Palmas de Gran Canaria. In 1983 Spantax dropped the somewhat drab livery that it had used for many years, in favour of a dramatically improved new image. The triple cheatlines of light blue, red and dark blue commenced as a wedge under the cockpit windows, and underlined the unique dark blue Spantax logo. The tail-fin displayed a most ingenious motif which very successfully combined the 'S' initial in blue, with a bright dayglo orange globe. Onto this was superimposed a white 'paper dart'. It should be noted that the motif was totally reversed on the

starboard side, except for the dart which always pointed forward. Additional motifs were sometimes carried on the engines, but were placed to match the direction of the tail motif on each side. On March 29, 1988, Spantax suspended all operations, following the collapse of refinancing talks. At that time, the airline's fleet consisted of two McDonnell Douglas MD83s (EC-EFF and EC-EFK), two Douglas DC-10-10s (N52UA and N917JW), one Douglas DC-8-61 (EC-DVC), and a Boeing 737-200 (EC-EEG). Prior to the carrier's demise there were talks about the purchase of the two Boeing 767-209s from China Airlines, although this deal was not completed. Other examples were sought, although the operation of this type never took place with the airline. Just before Spantax's cessation, it had been chartering capacity from other airlines, including Boeing 747s from Tower Air, Douglas DC-10-30s from Malaysian Airlines System, and Boeing 707s from Middle East Airlines. The carrier's ICAO call sign was 'SPANTAX'. *(K. G. Wright)*

SPANTAX (BX/BXS)　　　　　　　　　　　Spain

Formed in 1959, this Spanish carrier operated charters for the IT market in Europe and to North and South America. It was primarily for the latter destinations that a Douglas DC-10-30 was acquired in October 1978. Registered EC-DEG, its first service took place on November 21 when it left Palma bound for Madrid and New York (JFK). Subsequently its utilization included regular missions from Helsinki and Stockholm to Las Palmas. as well as operations to Los Angeles, Tokyo (NRT), and Mexico. All this came to an end on September 13, 1982, when the aircraft crashed at Malaga. With a full load of 380 passengers, the DC-10 commenced its take-off roll. At about the halfway point, a decision was taken to abort the flight, however, it was not able to stop within the available length, and in the end overran the runway by a considerable distance. In the process the aircraft wrecked four cars and a truck, as it careered across the main road, losing its undercarriage as it ploughed through a stone wall. A concrete building removed the starboard engine whilst the remainder of the airframe demolished a two-storey house, before it finally came to a halt. It was hardly surprising that fire broke out in the wing, quickly spreading to the still-intact fuselage which eventually was completely destroyed. All of the 56 people killed in the accident were travelling in the rear cabin, where the two doors failed to open due to bad distortion suffered during the last stages of the crash. Once the flight recorder had been analysed it was apparent that there had been neither structural or engine failure in any way. Vibration experienced on the flightdeck had prompted the decision to abandon the run, but it was taken too late to safely pull up in the distance remaining. Following this accident a similar machine was leased to take over the outstanding commitments. This aircraft remained with Spantax until the spring of 1984, when it was replaced by a third example. This time the new arrival was one of the original Swissair aircraft (HB-IHB), but was re-registered for its Spanish career as EC-DUG. Configured for its new role with 352 seats, it served the airline until 1986, when it was sold to Continental Airlines in October. For the winter operations, an ex-World Airways Series 10, was leased, as EC-EAZ. This however, did not last long, as the aircraft was later sold in the USA. Seen here at Stockholm is EC-EAZ, operating a flight to Las Palmas. *(K. G. Wright)*

SUN COUNTRY AIRLINES (SY/SCX)

United States of America

Sun Country Airlines is a Minneapolis/St Paul-based charter carrier. It was formed in 1982 following the collapse of Braniff International, by a group of former Braniff employees. Operations began on January 20, 1983, when the airline commenced IT services within the mainland USA, using a sole Boeing 727-200. This was however supplemented by leased aircraft of the same type, when required. When more capacity became necessary in June 1986, Sun Country took delivery of a Douglas DC-10-40, N144JC, on lease from Northwest Airlines. Prior to its introduction into service, the aircraft was given a 370 seat all economy/coach layout for its new role. This involved flights, on behalf of MLT Tours, to vacation cities and resorts throughout Florida, California, Mexico, and the Caribbean. Generally, services originated from cities such as Dallas, Denver, San Francisco and, of course, its home base at Minneapolis/St Paul. The present fleet consists of several Boeing 727-200 Advanced, and the sole Douglas DC-10-40. Additional capacity is leased-in during the peak season. Sun Country's Boeing 727s sport a livery which features a bright orange windowline, which is trimmed above in red and below in yellow. This flows from the cockpit windows along the fuselage and finally sweeps up onto the fin, where it is surmounted by an orange and red sun motif. However, the DC-10 wears an even more striking livery. This is still red, orange, and yellow, but now has the sun on the fuselage at the head of the triple cheatlines, which are broken to accommodate huge orange 'Sun Country' titles. Seen here at its home base is N144JC, the aircraft having just undergone maintenance. The aircraft was built in 1972 and was delivered to Northwest Airlines the same year, as N144US. This DC-10 is powered by three Pratt and Whitney JT9D-20 engines, has the construction number 46753, and the serial number 66. The carrier's ICAO call sign is 'SUN COUNTRY'. *(K. G. Wright)*

SWISSAIR (SR/SWR) Switzerland

Swissair was formed on March 26, 1931, when Ad Astra Aero and Basle Air Transport were amalgamated. The former company was founded in 1919, and began flying boat operations in Switzerland, before pioneering international routes. Today Swissair operates an extensive network of scheduled passenger and cargo services linking 107 cities in 72 countries, in Europe, North and South America, Africa, the Middle and·Far East. The airline has a number of aviation-related subsidiaries, including Balair, CTA, and Swissair Associated companies. It also owns catering, hotel, tourism, real estate and insurance firms. Swissair is a partner with SAS, KLM, and UTA in the KSSU consortium, which was formed to co-operate in technical and equipment pooling. When this group announced its combined order for the DC-10 in 1969, Swissair was the first to specify the exact number required. It was over three years later when, at a joint ceremony at Long Beach on November 21, 1972, the carrier received its first Series 30 in company with fellow KSSU member KLM. During the Spring of 1988, the Swiss national flag carrier became the first airline to put the Fokker 100 into commercial service. It was also the initial company to operate the Airbus A310-322 Intercontinental, in February 1986. Approximately 78 per cent of share capital is held by private interests and the rest by public institutions. A fleet of DC-10, MD11, MD81, Fokker 100, and Boeing 747 aircraft is maintained. It should be noted that some scheduled passenger flights are operated on behalf of Swissair, by Crossair, using Saab 340A equipment. The livery worn by the former carrier is bold. A Swiss flag covers the tail, boldly stating the airline's country of origin. This is complemented by bright red 'Swissair' titles over a white fuselage top. Straight twin cheatlines in brown (upper) and black (lower) extend from nose to tail below the window level. The lower fuselage is finished in grey on the A310s, whilst natural metal appears on the other types, some of which are highly polished. Seen here is a DC-10-30, whilst taxiing at Zurich. The carrier's ICAO call sign is 'SWISSAIR'. *(K. G. Wright)*

THAI AIRWAYS
INTERNATIONAL (TG/THA)

Thailand

Thai International was founded in 1959 as joint venture between Thailand's domestic carrier, Thai Airways Company, and Scandinavian Airlines System. The latter company initially provided operations, managerial and marketing expertise, with training assistance aimed at building a fully independent national airline within the shortest possible time. In 1960, flights were inaugurated to nine overseas destinations, all within the Asian region. Intercontinental services were launched in 1971 to Australia, followed by flights to Europe in 1972. The first aircraft used by Thai were Douglas DC-6Bs. Subsequently the fleet utilized Convair 990 Coronados, Sud Aviation SE-210 Caravelles (with which Thai was able to offer the first all-jet fleet of any Asian airline), Douglas DC-9s and DC-8s. The fleet was gradually standardized using the examples of the latter type; first the Series 33, with 140 seats; the Series 62, with 146 seats; then the Series 63, with 200 seats. Wide-bodied Douglas DC-10s were introduced in 1975, followed two years later by the Airbus Industrie A300; and in 1979 by the Boeing 747. Thai International's growth was greatly accelerated on April 1, 1988, as a result of its merger with

Thai Airways Company, the domestic airline. Today, Thai serves from its Bangkok base 23 domestic cities, and 47 international cities in 36 countries. A fleet of Douglas DC-10, Airbus Industrie A300, A310, Boeing 737, 747, Shorts 330 and 360, and BAe 146 aircraft is maintained. The carrier is one of the world's largest operators of the Airbus A300/310, and increased its fleet further when additional A300-600s were delivered in 1989. These aircraft are utilized on the airline's regional routes. As for the domestic operations, Thai has been leasing an extra Boeing 737, which has also been used to supplement regional routes such as Saigon and Brunei. Two BAe 146-300s were introduced in August partly to replace the older aircraft. The Douglas DC-10-30 seen here was in fact on lease from Air Afrique. It was only registered TU-TAM for a short time with Thai, before it reverted to being HS-TGB. Delivered on June 28, 1975, as 'Sriwanna', the aircraft stayed with Thai for approximately eleven months, before being returned to its owners. The carrier's ICAO call sign is 'THAI INTER'. *(Thai Airways International)*

TRANS INTERNATIONAL AIRLINES (TIA)

United States of America

Trans International Airlines was formed on December 20, 1948, with a base at Oakland, California, as Los Angeles Air Service; a CAB certificate was subsequently issued on July 8, 1949. To avoid confusion with Los Angeles Airways, the carrier changed its name on July 18, 1960, to Trans International Airways. The following year it was decided to cease individual ticketing, thus allowing the travel agent to do the work for the airline. June 22, 1962 saw the company become the first supplemental jet operator, when it took delivery of its first Douglas DC-8 equipment. In October of that year, TIA was purchased by Studebaker Corporation. It was then sold again two years later, this time to Kirk Kerkorian. The Chairman had great faith in the DC-8 (as did most other supplemental carriers), and with this in mind, he placed an order for a large quantity of this aircraft type, with which the airline went from strength to strength. On April 5, 1966, the carrier was granted licenses to operate transatlantic flights, followed on September 30 by flights to the Pacific and Latin America. During the months that followed. TIA settled down to a steady existence, and developed extensive business in contracts of all kinds, including affinity tour groups and inclusive tours. 1967 proved to be a good year for the airline. Profits in excess of $2 million were made, and with daily utilization of aircraft totalling over 12 hours, this was hardly surprising. TIA became a public company on June 28 of that year, and the Transamerica Corporation acquired control of the carrier on February 23, 1968. As of December 31, 1969, the carrier operated a fleet of two Boeing 727-100s, and eight Douglas DC-8-61/63s. The former type was frequently used on TIA's Oakland to Hawaii service, with N1728T, a -171C, being the second 727 to enter service with the company. Douglas DC-10s were acquired, and the first of these entered service on April 27, 1973. An opportunity was forthcoming in 1976 for the carrier to take over Saturn Airways, another charter airline. Talks progressed well, with the final purchase being made on November 30 of that year. October 1, 1979 saw a change of name to Transamerica, with scheduled services beginning a month later. Boeing 747 equipment joined the fleet in December of that year. *(B. J. Eagles)*

TURK HAVA YOLLARI (TK/THY)   Turkey

THY was formed by the Turkish Government in May 1933 as Devolet Hava Yollari. It operated under this title for nearly twenty-six years until February 1956, when the airline became a private corporation. Today, THY operates scheduled passenger services connecting Ankara, Istanbul, Antalaya, Izmir, and Adana, with eleven other domestic points. An extensive network of international scheduled services to Europe, the Middle East, North Africa, and the Far East is also operated. Charter flights to the Federal Republic of Germany are also undertaken. THY subsidiaries are USAS (Ground Handling Corporation), Kibris Turk Hava Yollari (Cyprus Airlines), BHT (Bogayiei Air Transport Corporation), and Havas (Airport Ground Handling Corporation). A fleet of Douglas DC-10, DC-9, Boeing 707, 727, and Airbus A310 aircraft is maintained. One of the carrier's two DC-10s can be seen here whilst on approach to London's Heathrow Airport on September 8, 1973. The aircraft,

TC-JAU and TC-JAY, both Series 10s, were delivered new to the airline from the manufacturer. There was a third example, TC-JAV, but this DC-10 crashed near Paris, on March 4, 1974. The current THY livery is made up of the red and white national colours, in a stylized pinstripe form. Five narrow red lines form the cheatline, which separates the white upper fuselage from the grey undersides. This terminates in a distinctive black anti-dazzle panel at the nose. A band of six broad stripes covers most of the tail fin, interrupted only by a white disk, which displays the traditional THY bird logo. A long title arrangement takes up most of the upper fuselage with the black letters reading 'Turk Hava Yollari — Turkish Airlines THY', followed by the national flag. The Turkish variant appears before the English on both sides. The carrier's ICAO call sign is 'TURKAIR'.
(Aviation Photo News)

UNITED AIRLINES (UA/UAL)

United States of America

United Airlines was formed on March 27, 1931, as the management company of four pioneer airlines: Boeing Air Transport, Pacific Air Transport, National Air Transport, and Varney Airlines (founded in 1926). Capital Airlines was absorbed in 1961. United became a subsidiary of UAL Inc, a holding company, in 1969. The company played a vital part in the existence of the Douglas DC-10, since had it not ordered twenty-five examples of the aircraft, it is unlikey that the type would ever have been built. Its order certainly launched the DC-10, which has been a prominent member of United's fleet since the first was delivered in July 1971. Having been beaten by American Airlines for the honour of operating the first commercial DC-10 service, the carrier introduced it on August 14,1971, when N1802U was given the San Francisco — Washington sector. Today, the airline is one of the world's largest carriers, having completed the purchase of Pan Am's Pacific division on February 10, 1986. Under the terms of the agreement, United took over eighteen aircraft, spare parts, property, facilities and about 2600 Pan Am employees associated with the Pacific division. In June 1986, United established formal feeder agreements with three US regional carriers, namely Air Wisconsin, Aspen Airways, and West Air; all of which operate under the banner 'United Express'. In January of the following year, United purchased the Hilton International hotel chain. The airline operates an extensive system of scheduled passenger and cargo routes linking more than 160 cities in the United States, Canada, and Mexico. International services are operated to the Far East, Australasia and the Caribbean. Through a number of agreements with major airlines, United operates a system of code sharing. This enables airlines such as Alitalia and British Airways to fly to any point within the United States on one flight number, even though it is necessary to change planes en route. A fleet of Boeing 727, 737, 747, 757, 767, and Douglas DC-10 aircraft is maintained. An order for a quantity of the Boeing 747-400 type is outstanding for delivery from the early 'nineties. UAL subsidiaries include Westin Hotels, Hilton International, Hertz Car Rental, GAB Business Services, and Mauna Kea Properties. Douglas DC-10-30, N1854U, can be seen here in July 1988 at Honolulu International. The aircraft was originally delivered to Laker Airways in March 1980 as G-BGXG. It was repossessed by Douglas in April 1982, when Laker ceased operations, before being sold in September 1984 to United Airlines. The carrier's ICAO call sign is 'UNITED'. *(B. T. Richards)*

UNITED STATES AIR FORCE

Unites States of America

Since the days of the SAC KC-135 units, the USAF had turned its thoughts to a new form of tanker. Military Airlift Command was also becoming more dependent upon flight refuelling. Originally it was intended that the principal use for any new aircraft would be for the support of the bomber force, but by the mid-1970s further deliberations had conceived the idea of a tanker with the ability to also serve as a large capacity tanker. With the requirements finalized, the authorities approached likely manufacturers with an invitation to submit proposals. Only Boeing and McDonnell Douglas in the end qualified, since Lockheed had not proceeded with a variant of the Tristar. After evaluating the 747 and DC-10, it was announced on December 19, 1977, that Lockheed had won. An initial contract was signed for two aircraft, designated the KC-10A Extender, with production being given the go ahead nearly twelve months later. A follow-up contract calling for an additional four aircraft was signed in November 1979. Deliveries were to be phased through to 1987, by which time a requirement of 60 aircraft was forecast. The KC-10 dispenses fuel to its 'customers' by means of a fuelling boom, which is greatly advanced from that of the KC-135, having incorporated greater lateral and elevational control, increased length and greater transfer control. Unlike any other tanker, the KC-10A is equipped with hose and drogue systems, giving it the flexibility to allow simultaneous refuelling of both types on the same mission. The first aircraft, 79-0433, took to the skies on July 12, 1980, and became the first to be delivered to the USAF. Seen here is an example of one of the many KC-10A Extenders in service with the United States Air Force. It is depicted whilst on approach to USAFB Lakenheath in April 1988. *(K. G. Wright)*

UTA — UNION DE TRANSPORTS AERIENS (UT/UTA)

France

UTA was formed on October 1, 1963, following the amalgamation of Union Aéromaritime de Transport (UAT), and Compagnie de Transport Aérien Intercontinental. The former was founded in November 1949 by the French Shipping line, Compagnie Maritime de Chargeurs Réunis and other interests, and operated services to the former French Territories in West Africa, together with a route to Saigon. TAI however, was formed in June 1946 as a charter company, and in 1956 took over the former Air France routes to Australia and New Caledonia. Today, UTA is France's largest independent airline. It operates scheduled passenger and cargo services from Paris (CDG), Nice, Marseille, Lyon, and Toulouse, to over twenty-three points in Africa; to Bahrain and Muscat in the Middle East, to Los Angeles, San Francisco, and Honolulu in the USA, and to Tokyo (NRT) and eight other points in the Asia-Pacific region. Charter and inclusive-tour services are also provided. UTA is a subsidiary of Chargeurs Réunis, which has a 62.5 per cent holding. Companies in which the carrier has a shareholding include SODETRAF, Air Inter, CRMA, Revima, UTH (hotels), Compagnie

Aéromaritime d'Affrètement, UTA Services Tahiti (airport services), and holiday villages in Polynesia and New Caledonia. A fleet of Douglas DC-10, and Boeing 747 aircraft is utilized. An order for the Airbus A340 is anticipated for delivery from the early 'nineties. The carrier was one of the first airlines to adopt a modern white overall fuselage colouring, which in this case features passenger doors highlighted in bright green. The whole fin and rear of the fuselage is in dark blue, with a small white 'UTA' logo inconspicuously appearing at the top of the tail. Huge fuselage titles in dark blue are so large that they are often readable from the ground of an overflying aircraft. Pure freight aircraft have an all-white body without the green highlights, but wear additional blue cargo titles. The Boeing 747 is, however, the only pure freight plane in the fleet. Douglas DC-10-30, F-BTDB, can be seen here just prior to delivery. It should be noted that the aircraft was wearing its test registration number, N1341U. The airline's ICAO call sign is 'UTA'.

(UTA — French Airlines)

VARIG — BRAZILIAN AIRLINES (RG/VRG)

Brazil

Varig was founded in May 1927, with the technical assistance of the German Condor syndicate, for the operation of local services using a Dornier WAL flying boat. The first route was that between Porto Alegre and Rio Grande. The company subsequently absorbed several other airlines, including the domestic operator, Aero Geral (1951), the Real consortium (1961), and Panair do Brasil's equipment and international routes, in 1965. Today, Varig operates an extensive network of routes throughout South and Central America, as well as to the USA, Europe, Africa, and Japan. Domestic carriers Cruzeiro (acquired in 1975) and Rio-Sul are subsidiaries. Most of the company's shares are held by the foundation of employees and executives. A fleet of Douglas DC-10-30, Boeing 707-320C, 727-100, 737-200 and -300, 747-200B and -300, 767-200ER, Lockheed L-188 Electra, and Airbus A300B4 aircraft is operated. An order for a quantity of the McDonnell Douglas MD11P is anticipated for a 1990 delivery, thus enabling the airline to replace its older and less efficient sisters. The Lockheed Electra is still maintained on the

famous Ponte Area/Air Shuttle flights, between Rio de Janeiro and São Paulo. However, it is anticipated that these aircraft will be replaced by the faster and more fuel efficient Boeing 737-300. The Varig livery is predominantly dark blue. This is obtained from the national flag, and is the colour used for the broad cheatline, which curves round under the aircraft's chin, and also features a 'seam effect', that is created by white pinstripes at window level. The now famous company logo, a compass, is displayed on the fin, above black 'Varig' titles. However, on the fuselage, the company name is repeated in blue, alongside the Brazilian flag, and 'Brasil' lettering in black. The livery has been adopted to suit the shapes of the other aircraft. However, the only variation is the application of a 'flying figurehead' logo above the cheatline on the 747s, but within it on all other types. Underside colours vary, with those of the Douglas DC-10s and 747s in a natural metal, and the A300s in grey, whilst some DC-10s have a more attractive white applied. The carrier's ICAO call sign is 'VARIG'. *(Varig — Brazilian Airlines)*

VIASA — VENEZUELAN INTERNATIONAL AIRWAYS (VA/VIA)

Venezuela

In January 1961, the Venezuelan Government introduced a policy to rationalize the country's air services. Thus, Viasa was formed to take over the international routes of Avensa and LAV, although the former company retained a 25 per cent stake in the new airline. Scheduled passenger and freight operations began in the April of that year. Today, Viasa operates scheduled passenger services from Caracas, Maracaibo, Porlamar, and Barcelona, across the Atlantic to Lisbon, Oporto, Santiago de Compostela, Madrid, Zurich, Paris (ORY), Milan, Rome, London (LHR), Frankfurt and Amsterdam. The carrier's network also includes Miami, New York (JFK), Houston, San Juan, Bogota, Quito, Lima, Santiago, Rio de Janeiro, Buenos Aires, Curaçao, Aruba, and Santo Domingo. Charters are operated to Toronto and Vancouver during the winter season. Viasa also dry-leases 747F capacity from Federal Express for services to Miami and New York (JFK). The carrier is wholly owned by the Venezuelan Government. A fleet of Douglas DC-10 and Airbus Industrie A300 aircraft is maintained. An order for several McDonnell Douglas MD11 types will replace the former, once they begin to arrive in the early 'nineties. The latest Viasa livery includes two minor changes to the traditional image that has been utilised by the company for some years. A new blue cheatline follows a modern trend and now appears below the windows. This allows for an extended white cabin roof effectively to add life to the scheme. The somewhat disjointed 'seven stars' have been omitted from behind the cockpit windows, giving space for the orange 'Viasa' logo, which has been moved forward into a more prominent positon. Blue 'Venezuela' lettering is displayed over the wings, another move forward, but the characteristic orange fin remains the same, with its white 'Viasa' logo and Venezuelan flag near the top of the rudder. Seen here is one of the Venezuelan flag carrier's Douglas DC-10 aircraft, landing at Caracas, after its flight from London (LHR), as VA 701. The carrier's ICAO call sign is 'VIASA'.

(Viasa — Venezuelan Airlines)

WARDAIR CANADA (WD/WDA)   Canada

Wardair can trace its history back to 1946, when Maxwell W. Ward started bush operations from Yellowknife, as the Polaris Charter Company. The company utilized a single De Havilland Fox Moth, which was used to fly charters in support of the rapidly developing mining industry in the Northwest Territories. Wardair was formed in 1953 to continue this work, and began operations using an Otter. The name, Wardair Canada, was adopted in 1962, and operating authority amended to include international charter operations. The airline went public in 1967 and the major shareholder was Maxwell W. Ward, who owned 31 per cent of the equity and 57 per cent of the voting power. On January 1, 1976, the name was changed to Wardair Canada (1975), with Wardair International Ltd becoming a parent company to the airline operations as well as to wholly-owned subsidiaries: Wardair (Holidays) Inc, Wardair (UK), Wardair Hawaii, Wardair, Wardair Equipment, and Redrock Reinsurance, France SARL. An interesting move came about in 1989, when Canadian Airlines International took over the carrier. Although

operating at first as a separate entity, the two forces subsequently merged to become one airline. Prior to the take-over, the Wardair fleet consisted of Boeing 747, Airbus Industrie A310, and DHC-6 Twin Otter types. An order was outstanding for the McDonnell Douglas MD88 and Fokker 100, but these aircraft were not received, and were sold to other carriers. Although formerly a charter operator, Wardair launched its first domestic and international scheduled services in 1986. At that time the carrier ordered twelve A310s to replace its fleet of Douglas DC-10s and Airbus A300s. Prior to its demise, the Canadian airline operated domestic scheduled services between Toronto and Calgary, Edmonton, Ottawa, Montreal, Vancouver, and Winnipeg. International scheduled services were flown from Vancouver, Calgary, Edmonton, Toronto and Ottowa to London (LGW and STN), Cardiff, Birmingham, Leeds/Bradford, Newcastle, Prestwick (PIK), and Manchester, and from Montreal to San Juan (Puerto Rico) and Puerto Plata (Dominican Republic). The airline's ICAO call sign was 'WARDAIR'. *(Wardair Canada)*

WESTERN AIRLINES (WA/WAL)

United States of America

Western Airlines can trace its history back to July 13, 1925, to the foundation in Sacramento of one of the country's pioneer airlines, Western Air Express, which had obtained a mail contract over the Los Angeles-Salt Lake City, via Las Vegas, route. This service was inaugurated on April 17, 1926 with Douglas M-2s, followed by the first passenger flights on May 23. Following the amalgamation with T.A.T. to form Transcontinental & Western Air (T.W.A.) on July 16, 1930, W.A.E. continued as a separate entity, and for a few months in 1934 took the name General Airlines. However, the merger was dissolved later that year, following post office cancellations of mail contracts. W.A.E. went on to become Western Air Lines and Transcontinental became Trans World Airlines. The title, Western Airlines was adopted on March 11, 1941. Western operations were expanded across the Rocky Mountains in 1944, following the acquisition of Inland Airlines. Jet services were introduced in 1960, thus allowing Western to compete on equal terms with the major carriers. In July 1967 Western absorbed Pacific Northern Airlines (PNA) to add over 3300 miles of routes to its system, including lines into Alaska. In 1961 Western unsuccessfully attempted to conclude a merger with Continental Airlines, which in the end was acquired by the Texas Air Corporation. Plans for a merger with Wien Air Alaska were dropped in 1983. 1987 saw the take-over of the carrier, by Atlanta-based Delta Air Lines. Prior to that, Western operated scheduled passenger and cargo services over a wide network concentrated in western states, and reached as far as Anchorage, Fairbanks, Juneau, and Ketchikan (Alaska); Vancouver, Edmonton and Calgary (Canada); Honolulu (Hawaii); Acapulco, Guadalajara, Ixtapa/Zihuatanejo, Mexico City, Maztalin and Puerto Vallarta (Mexico), Washington D.C. and New York City. A fleet of Douglas DC-10-10, Boeing 727-200, 737-200, and 737-300 aircraft were operated prior to the take-over. An order for several Boeing 767-200s were on order, but were subsequently cancelled. Seen here is a DC-10-10 on departure from Honolulu International Airport, the aircraft's final destination being Los Angeles. The carrier's ICAO call sign was 'WESTERN'. *(K. G. Wright)*

WORLD AIRWAYS
(WO/WOA)

United States of America

World Airways commenced operations on March 29, 1949 as a small US charter airline. The following year the carrier was purchased by Edward J. Daly (who owned 81 per cent of the shareholding until his death in January 1984), and quickly became a leading supplemental charter carrier. CAB approval for low-cost, coast-to-coast scheduled services was granted in early 1979, with intercontinental flights linking New York (EWR) and Baltimore/Washington D.C. with Los Angeles and Oakland, commencing on April 12. Scheduled services to Honolulu, London (LGW) and Frankfurt, were added in 1981. Worldwide passenger and cargo charters were also flown under contract to the United States Military Airlift Command. The World Airways fleet consists entirely of Douglas DC-10-10 and DC-10-30 aircraft. On March 21, 1986, the carrier unveiled its dramatic new image, which replaced a traditional red and gold 'flying globe' livery. A pure white-overall fuselage sports high visibility 'World'

titles in a purpose-designed, sloping burgundy lettering, with the first stroke of the 'W' in a deep blue. The 'W' initial itself becomes the company motif on the fin, above a repeat of the fuselage titles on the third engine. During September 1986, World closed down all of its scheduled services, which accounted for the bulk of operations. A total of 1500 employees were laid off, and the airline sold off its fleet of Boeing 727 airliners. The carrier now concentrates solely on worldwide passenger and cargo charters, and has the provision of overhaul facilities at its Oakland base. Seen here on arrival at Hong Kong's Kai Tak Airport on October 7, 1987, is Douglas DC-10-30F (CF), N106WA. The aircraft was at the time on lease to Malaysian Airline System, as can be seen by the hybrid livery that the type is sporting. This particular machine was built in 1979, and is powered by three General Electric CF6-50C2 engines. The airline's ICAO call sign is 'WORLD'. *(B. J. Eagles)*